THE NONPROFIT ENTERPRISE IN MARKET ECONOMICS

T0316335

Routledge
Taylor & Francis Group

LONDON AND NEW YORK

FUNDAMENTALS OF PURE AND APPLIED ECONOMICS

EDITORS IN CHIEF

J. LESOURNE, Conservatoire National des Arts et Métiers, Paris, France

H. SONNENSCHEIN, University of Pennsylvania, Philadelphia, PA, USA

ADVISORY BOARD

K. ARROW, Stanford, CA, USA
W. BAUMOL, Princeton, NJ, USA
W. A. LEWIS, Princeton, NJ, USA
S. TSURU, Tokyo, Japan

ECONOMIC SYSTEMS & COMPARATIVE ECONOMICS I
In 3 Volumes

THE NONPROFIT
ENTERPRISE IN MARKET
ECONOMICS

ESTELLE JAMES AND
SUSAN ROSE-ACKERMAN

Routledge
Taylor & Francis Group

LONDON AND NEW YORK

First published in 1986 by
Harwood Academic Publishers GmbH

Reprinted in 2001 by
Routledge

2 Park Square, Milton Park, Abingdon, Oxon, OX14 4RN
Simultaneously published in the USA and Canada by Routledge

711 Third Avenue, New York, NY 10017

Transferred to Digital Printing 2007

Routledge is an imprint of the Taylor & Francis Group, an informa business

First issued in paperback 2013

The publishers have made every effort to contact authors/copyright holders
of the works reprinted in *Harwood Fundamentals of Pure & Applied Economics*.
This has not been possible in every case, however, and we would welcome
correspondence from those individuals/companies we have been unable to
trace.

These reprints are taken from original copies of each book. in many cases
the condition of these originals is not perfect. the publisher has gone to
great lengths to ensure the quality of these reprints, but wishes to point
out that certain characteristics of the original copies will, of necessity, be
apparent in reprints thereof.

British Library Cataloguing in Publication Data
A CIP catalogue record for this book
is available from the British Library

The Nonprofit Enterprise in Market Economics

ISBN 978-0-415-27466-1 (hbk)
ISBN 978-0-415-86627-9 (pbk)

The Nonprofit Enterprise in Market Economics

Estelle James
State University of New York at Stony Brook, USA

and

Susan Rose-Ackerman
Columbia University School of Law, USA

A volume in the Economic Systems section
edited by
J. M. Montias
Yale University
and
J. Kornai
Institute of Economics, Hungarian Academy of Sciences

hp
dp harwood academic publishers
chur · london · paris · new york

© 1986 by Harwood Academic Publishers GmbH
Poststrasse 22, 7000 Chur, Switzerland

Harwood Academic Publishers

P.O. Box 197
London WC2E 9PX
England

58, rue Lhomond
75005 Paris
France

P.O. Box 786
Cooper Station
New York, NY 10276
United States of America

Library of Congress Cataloging-in-Publication Data

James, Estelle.
The nonprofit enterprise in market economics.

(Fundamentals of pure and applied economics; v. 9. Economic systems section)
Bibliography: p.
Includes index.
1. Corporations, Nonprofit. I. Rose-Ackerman, Susan.
II. Title. III. Series: Fundamentals of pure and applied economics; v. 9. IV. Series: Fundamentals of pure and applied mathematics. Economics systems section.
HD62.6.J36 1986   658'.048   86-14940
ISBN 3-7186-0329-2

Contents

Introduction to the Series

Drawing on a personal network, an economist can still relatively easily stay well informed in the narrow field in which he works, but to keep up with the development of economics as a whole is a much more formidable challenge. Economists are confronted with difficulties associated with the rapid development of their discipline. There is a risk of "balkanisation" in economics, which may not be favorable to its development.

Fundamentals of Pure and Applied Economics has been created to meet this problem. The discipline of economics has been subdivided into sections (listed inside). These sections include short books, each surveying the state of the art in a given area.

Each book starts with the basic elements and goes as far as the most advanced results. Each should be useful to professors needing material for lectures, to graduate students looking for a global view of a particular subject, to professional economists wishing to keep up with the development of their science, and to researchers seeking convenient information on questions that incidentally appear in their work.

Each book is thus a presentation of the state of the art in a particular field rather than a step-by-step analysis of the development of the literature. Each is a high-level presentation but accessible to anyone with a solid background in economics, whether engaged in business, government, international organizations, teaching, or research in related fields.

Three aspects of *Fundamentals of Pure and Applied Economics* should be emphasized:

—First, the project covers the whole field of economics, not only theoretical or mathematical economics.

—Second, the project is open-ended and the number of books is not predetermined. If new interesting areas appear, they will generate additional books.

—Last, all the books making up each section will later be grouped to constitute one or several volumes of an Encyclopedia of Economics.

The editors of the sections are outstanding economists who have selected as authors for the series some of the finest specialists in the world.

J. Lesourne   *H. Sonnenschein*

The Nonprofit Enterprise in Market Economies

ESTELLE JAMES

Professor of Economics, S.U.N.Y., Stony Brook, NY, USA

SUSAN ROSE-ACKERMAN

Professor of Law and Political Economy, Columbia University School of Law, NY, USA

1. INTRODUCTION

In classical economic models no true institutions or choices exist. Competitive markets determine price. Cost and demand functions are known with certainty and determine quantity. Owners of firms are profit-maximizers who contract with inputs to produce outputs; inputs do not need to be motivated or monitored so long as they are paid the going wage; the firm itself is a black box.

Quite early in the development of modern economics, however, scholars recognized that the internal organization, incentive structure and behavior of firms were important independent topics of study and that simple models of profit maximization in competitive markets could not be used inside the firm. Similarly, when economists began to study the behavior of political institutions and public bureaucracies, profit maximizing models were inappropriate and social welfare maximization proved equally unsatisfactory as a positive model. More recently, economic analysts have started to

We wish to thank Richard Steinberg for his detailed and helpful comments and K. H. Lee for research assistance. We also wish to thank the Exxon Education Foundation, the National Endowment for the Humanities, and the Program on Nonprofit Organizations, Yale University, for their support on some of our research which is reported in this survey essay.

1

examine a broader variety of institutional forms which have been used in the historical past and are used today in many cultures. Even when their overall economic impact is small, the continued existence of these alternatives is an important source of evidence on the viability of substitutes for our dominant institutions. Thus, economists whose primary concern is the behavior of profit-maximizing firms in a competitive economy can benefit from the study of alternatives such as nonprofit corporations, consumer or producer cooperatives, labor-managed firms, partnerships, bureaucracies and public enterprises, and a large literature has developed on these topics. This literature forces us to consider a wider set of actors, interactions and decisions, than can be accommodated in simple classical models.

Since the other institutional forms are discussed elsewhere in these volumes, we concentrate here on an analysis of the private nonprofit organization (NPO) which has no owners with a legal right to appropriate the surplus generated by the organization. Economic analyses of nonprofit firms can generate insights both for those whose primary interest is the voluntary nonprofit sector and for economists whose main concern is the private market economy. A sensitivity to the opportunities for private gain even within nominally charitable organizations leads to a focus on the decision-making structure and incentives within nonprofit firms. Conversely, an understanding of the independent role of trust and altruism can inform our understanding of organizations supposedly concerned only with profit maximization.

In many parts of the world the nonprofit form existed long before the modern corporation. However, the fact that total income and output generated by for-profit corporations now by far exceeds that of nonprofit organizations suggests that such corporations have a strong comparative advantage in modern economies. Nevertheless, the survival of NPO's through centuries of economic change and across most societies suggests that they, too, have a comparative advantage for producing certain services. A central question then is, which services and why? Who is willing to establish nonprofit organizations and what goals do the founders and managers have? How do nonprofits overcome their disadvantage vis-a-vis the for-profit corporation and how do they behave in the face of competition from both for-profits and government enterprises? Tentative answers to these questions are beginning to emerge from current research but because of the diversity of managerial goals and funding sources in the sector, no single, simple paradigm is likely to result.

Thus, after summarizing the available data on the size, activity and funding sources of the nonprofit sector in Part II, we turn to a three-pronged analysis of nonprofit behavior in Parts III, IV and V. Parts III and IV are sharply contrasting. In the former we present the most important normative justifications for nonprofit organizations developed by economic analysts. These researchers assume that the nondistribution constraint produces desirable behavior in the face of markets with information imperfections or private demands for collective goods. In the latter we work through a series of models that contrast NPO behavior with the behavior of profit making organizations (PMO's) in a competitive market. We show that, compared with this benchmark, NPO's may choose an inefficient mix of inputs or outputs and may oversupply quality. Thus in industries where competitive PMO's can survive there appears to be no affirmative argument for encouraging nonprofit production. How can these two contrasting positions be reconciled?

In Part V we argue that, while each has produced valuable insights, both are caricatures of the nonprofit sector. The former is overly idealized; the latter, overly cynical. Instead, we propose a way of thinking about nonprofit firms that incorporates elements of both approaches but emphasizes the independent role of ideology as a fundamental justification for NPO existence and a basic explanation of their behavior. In Parts VI and VII we go on to contrast nonprofits with profit-constrained firms and public bureaucracies, respectively. The paper concludes in Part VIII with an analysis of some major policy issues.

2. SOME EMPIRICAL OBSERVATIONS: THE SCOPE OF THE NONPROFIT SECTOR

Before moving to an evaluation of the existing theoretical and empirical studies, it is well to get a sense of the scope of the sector.

We begin by defining nonprofits (NPO's) in their basic legal-structural sense as "private organizations that are prohibited from distributing a monetary residual." Such organizations are found throughout the world and, in different variations, have been amply studied by economists and other social scientists. Included in this definition, for example, are political parties, interest groups, labor unions, trade associations, insurance companies and private clubs.

This category, obviously, is far too broad to cover in a single essay, or even a single volume. Much of the discussion of the nonprofit sector and nonprofit theory in the recent American literature, therefore, focuses on a subset of organizations that are tax-exempt and eligible to receive tax-deductible gifts under Section 501(c)(3) of the Internal Revenue Code. These organizations combine three important attributes: (1) they are legally and structurally nonprofit; (2) they provide "socially useful" services; and (3) they are philanthropies, deriving a portion of their revenues from (tax deductible) contributions. In this essay, we are primarily concerned with these service-providing, philanthropic organizations, which, as a group, generate about 5% of national income and 9% of employment in the United States (including the value of volunteer time; see Hodgkinson and Weitzman, 1984, p. 9). However, many of the behavioral characteristics we derive would also apply to the broader set of NPO's mentioned above (with objective functions suitably redefined).

A broad picture of the current status of the service-providing nonprofit sector in the United States is presented in Tables I and II. The data are not entirely consistent because they use somewhat different sources and suffer from gaps and inaccuracies, but they do give a good general outline of major activities and sources of revenue. Table I combines 1980 data on operating nonprofits from an Urban Institute study with additional information on volunteer labor. Table II uses data compiled by Independent Sector from various sources. Expenditures in Table I are generally less than revenues in Table II at least in part because the revenue figures include contributions to endowment.

NPO's provide six broad types of services: health care, education and research, social service, arts and culture, community development, and religion. The health and education categories are by far the largest but since many of these institutions were started by religious organizations, the categories in Table I understate the role of religion. The theories of nonprofit formation and survival that we describe in Part III seek to explain why nonprofits are active in these six areas and not in others such as steelmaking and retail trade. Our discussion of entrepreneurship in Part V explores the importance of religious and other ideological motivations.

A distinctive feature of the sector is the substantial amount of funding (25% or more, the exact percentage varying with activity and data source) derived from private philanthropy. As we shall see, many nonprofit theories focus on this empirical observation, which seems to run counter to expected "free rider" behavior. It is important to recognize, however, that education, research and health care, which together account for over 70% of the sector (over 80% if religion is excluded), are only about 10% financed by monetary donations and receive more than half of their revenue from private fee-paying customers. In fact, philanthropy is heavily concentrated in the "religion" category and, leaving religion aside, we find a negative correlation between the size of a sub-sector and its dependence on private giving.

As is well known, volunteer labor is particularly difficult to measure. If the data in Table I are reliable, it appears that the value of volunteer labor is greater than but positively correlated with private monetary donations. Thus for many organizations, especially in social service, community development and the arts, volunteer labor is a major contributor to their well-being.

The tables indicate that government support accounts for 26 to 28% of sector revenues, approximately the same as private philanthropy. In the U.S. public support is most important for NPO's providing social services, community development aid and health care. Private education, on the other hand, has a relatively low level of dependence on public money. As we shall see, government support is even more important to nonprofits in other countries.

In most sub-sectors, public agencies and for-profit firms compete with nonprofits for funds and customers. Comparative cross-section data on the market shares of different types of firms are difficult to come by, but Tables III and IV summarize the available U.S. data. The pattern is roughly as follows. Except for certain vocational and technical schools and "white academies" in the South, most educational institutions are either nonprofit or public institutions,

TABLE I
Nonprofit expenditure and revenue by source, 1980

Type of nonprofit organization	(1) Total expenditures[1]	[$ billion] (2) Private philanthropy[1]	(3) Federal support[1]	Percentage of sector expenditure (4) Private philanthropy[6]	(5) Federal support[7]	(6) Other[8]	[$ billions] (7) Value of volunteer labor[9]	(8) Expenditures plus value of volunteer labor[13]	(9) Value of volunteer labor as % of (8)
Social service	13.2	4.7	6.5	36	49	15	13.2[10]	26.4	50
Community development/ civic	5.4	1.4	2.3	26	43	31	4.7[11]	10.1	47
Education & research	25.2	6.7	5.6	26	22	52	8.4	33.6	25
Health care	70.0	6.4	24.9	9	36	55	8.7	78.7	10
Arts & culture	2.6	3.0[3]	0.3	n.a.	12	n.a.	2.2	4.8	46
Religious	24.0[2]	22.2[4]	0	(92)[2]	0	(8)[2]	13.7	37.7	36
Total	140.4	44.5[5]	39.6[5]	25	28	50	55.6[12]	196.0	28

n.a. = not available.

1. Salamon and Abramson *The Federal Budget and the Nonprofit Sector*, Urban Institute, 1982. Expenditure data is based on IRS and Census Bureau figures supplemented with other data. The information on private giving is from AAFC, *Giving USA*, 1981.

2. Calculated using the estimate of private giving in column (2) and information from Independent Sector and Smith and Rosenbaum, "The Fiscal Capacity of the Voluntary Sector," (Mimeo, 1981), indicating that over 90% of the funds of religious organizations come from private gifts.

3. This figure reveals a problem with the AAFC data. It includes additions to endowment and gifts of appreciated property at their full value. Thus the level of gifts that can be used for current expenditures is overstated especially for education and culture.

4. Salamon and Abramson, Table 3. Data from AAFC, *Giving USA*, 1981.

5. Excludes "other." The omitted category accounted for $3.4 billion in gifts and $0.8 billion in Federal support to a mixture of organizations including foreign aid and technical assistance, international activities and education, and foundation endowment.

6. Column (2) as a percent of (1).

7. Column (3) as a percent of (1).

8. Other levels of government, fees, changes, etc. Calculated as a residual. Other government levels accounted for 5–10% with the balance of 35–40% from fees, charges and earned income.

9. Calculated by Weisbrod (1985, Table 8.7) from data in *America Volunteer* (Independent Sector). These numbers may be an overestimate because, according to Independent Sector only 90% of volunteers worked in the non-profit sector.

10. Includes social welfare, recreation, work-related programs, justice.

11. Includes "citizenship."

12. Includes general fundraising ($4.7 billion) not included in any subcategory. Political ($4.6 billion) and Community ($4.3 billion) are omitted.

13. This calculation is subject to error because the categories are not necessarily consistent.

TABLE II
Independent sector: Annual support by subsector and source: 1980

Type of nonprofit organization	[$ billion]					Percent of subsector revenues			
	(1) Total revenues	(2) Private giving	(3) Government	(4) Dues, fees and charges	(5) Endowment and other	(6) Private giving	(7) Government	(8) Dues, fees and charges	(9) Endowment and other
Social service[1]	16.2	4.9	5.6	4.0	1.7	30	35	25	11
Community development/ civic	5.5	1.4	2.0	1.5	0.6	25	36	27	11
Education & research	36.7	5.7	6.0	19.5	5.5	16	16	53	15
Health care	74.3	6.6	25.5	36.2	6.0	9	34	49	8
Arts & culture	5.0	3.1	1.2	0.5	0.2	62	24	10	4
Religious	18.0	15.5	0	—	2.5	86	0	—	13
Total	155.7[2]	43.9	40.3	61.7	9.8	28	26	40	6

Source: V. Hodgkinson and M. Weitzman, *Dimensions of the Independent Sector* (Independent Sector, 1984) Table 30.
[1] Includes legal service.
[2] Omits foundations.

with the latter predominating, especially for elementary and secondary education. Similarly, organizations serving the disadvantaged (e.g. in the social services) are mostly organized as nonprofits or government agencies. For-profits, however, sometimes provide services if an open-ended, fee-for-service public program exists with generous reimbursement rates. In health care the pattern is mixed and has changed rapidly in recent years because of the growth of public support under Medicare and Medicaid. In particular, in the nursing home and hospital industries, public subsidy has spurred the growth of for-profits. For culture and entertainment nonprofits are most important in areas with the smallest audience appeal, such as art museums, while for-profits predominate in areas with mass appeal such as radio and T.V. broadcasting. Thus, all three sectors operate in most industries, although one sector usually dominates (has more than half of total revenues and employment).

Tables III and IV also suggest the weakness of the basic categories. On the one hand, the distinction between public organizations and private nonprofits may be problematic for institutions like art museums which receive high levels of public support and, on the other hand, the nonprofit versus for-profit distinction may not be very useful for small break-even providers like many child-care centers. In the latter case, organizational form may result more from the details of state incorporation statutes and tax laws than from the advantages or disadvantages of the non-distribution constraint itself.

A somewhat different perspective is thrown on the role and scope of the nonprofit sector when we examine international data. In other countries, private philanthropy is generally not as important as it is in the United States, and tax laws differ, so we must modify our concept of the NPO, eliminating the emphasis on tax-deductible contributions. Instead, we make a distinction between service-providing organizations (such as schools and hospitals) and representational organizations (such as political parties, labor unions, trade associations and interest groups), and we define the NPO as a service organization that is prohibited from distributing a monetary residual. Unfortunately, most countries do not keep separate data on these organizations. In national income statistics, expenditures of NPO's are often grouped together with "household expenditures" and cannot be readily distinguished. A subset of expendi-

TABLE III

Service industries where taxable and tax-exempt firms co-exist U.S. Totals: Establishments with payroll, 1977[1]

SIC codes	Industry	Taxable		Tax-exempt[2]		Tax-exempt share of total	
		Number	Receipts[3] $1,000	Number	Expenses[4] $1,000	Number	Revenues[5]
7032	Sporting and recreational camps	2249	230,273	826	82,661	26.9	26.4
702, 704	Rooming houses and other lodging places[6]	3116	234,411	3096	219,861	49.8	48.4
7391	Commercial R & D Laboratories	1784	2,025,573	268	1,148,222	13.1	36.2
7397	Commercial testing laboratories	1924	686,010	178	66,171	8.5	8.8
Health:							
8051	Skilled nursing care facilities	5733	5,190,993	1258	1,615,259	18.0	23.7
8059	Nursing and personal care facilities	5046	2,003,888	1073	600,607	17.5	23.1
8062	General medical and surgical hospitals	779	4,281,837	3296	37,186,364	80.9	89.7
8063	Psychiatric hospitals	128	300,899	86	328,330	40.2	52.2
8069	Other specialty hospitals	79	161,153	242	1,681,961	75.4	91.3
803	Outpatient care facilities	3239	997,356	4178	1,805,082	56.3	64.4
Education:							
821	Elementary and secondary schools[7]	2237	273,109	3297	1,296,078	59.6	82.6
8221	Colleges, universities, professional schools and junior colleges	40	57,593	1537	11,730,047	97.5	99.5
8222	Junior colleges and technical inst.	101	93,040	218	297,581	68.3	76.2
823	Libraries and information centers	183	9,887	1386	178,358	88.3	94.7
824	Correspondence and vocational schools	2571	841,028	790	160,362	23.5	16.0
Social services:							
832	Individual and family social services	1986	201,524	12,440	2,236,902	86.2	91.7
833	Job training and vocational rehab. serv.	736	187,081	3396	1,048,367	82.2	84.9
835	Child day care services	14,172	759,554	10,641	829,218	42.9	52.2
836	Residential care	4600	666,042	5603	1,857,437	54.9	73.6
839	Social services	1610	224,267	8903	2,322,984	84.7	91.2
Culture, amusements and recreation:							
7922	Theatrical producers and misc. services	2713	917,336	651	206,312	19.4	18.4
929	Bands, orchestras, dance groups, actors, & other entertainers and groups.	4008	850,838	577	317,824	12.6	27.2

Sources: Summary Statistics for the United States: 1977, pp. 53-1-2, 53-1-3, in *U.S. Department of Commerce, Bureau of the Census, 1977 Census of Service Industries: Other Service Industries, SC77-A-53*, and *United States Report (Selected Service Industries)* SC77-A-52.

[1] For detailed definitions of terms, see the sources cited above.

[2] This includes nonprofit organizations, establishments owned by a government but operated by a private organization and agencies funded by government but operated independently (p. A-2).

[3] Receipts (basic dollar volume measure for taxable establishments) include receipts from customers or clients for services rendered and merchandise sold during 1977 whether or not payment was received in 1977, except for health practitioners, who reported on a cash basis (payments received regardless of when services were rendered), and educational institutions, which were instructed to report for the fiscal year ending in 1977. Total receipts do not include local and State sales taxes or Federal Excise taxes collected by the establishment directly from customers and paid directly by the establishment to a local, State, or Federal tax agency; nor do they include nonoperating income from such sources as investments, rental of real estate, etc. Receipts in this report do not include service receipts of manufacturers, wholesalers, retail establishments, or other businesses whose primary activity is other than service. They do, however, include receipts other than from services rendered (e.g. sales of merchandise to individuals or other business) by establishments primarily engaged in performing services covered in this segment of the census.

Rents and receipts of separately operated departments, concessions, etc. (e.g. a hospital gift shop, or a commercially operated university dormitory) are excluded. These operations would be classified according to their major activity and separately tabulated.

Although the count of establishments in this report represents the number in business at the end of the year, the receipts figures include receipts of all establishments in business at any time during the year.

[4] Expenses (basic dollar volume measure for tax-exempt organizations). Expenses include payroll, employee benefits, interest and rent, taxes, cost of supplies used for operation, depreciation expense, fees paid for fund-raising, and other expenses allocated to operations during 1977. (Educational institutions were instructed to report for the fiscal year ending in 1977).

Expenses in this report exclude outlays for purchase of real estate, construction and all other capital improvements, funds invested, assessments or dues paid to the parent or other chapters of the same organization, and funds transferred by fund-raising organizations to charities and other organizations.

[5] Tax-exempt establishments expenses divided by sum of receipts of taxable establishment and expenses of tax-exempt firms.

[6] Taxable firms include 702: Rooming and boarding houses, and 704: Organization hotels and lodging houses operated by membership organizations for the benefit of their constituents and not open to the general public. Non-profits are active only in sector 704 but may compete with organizations in 702. Sector 704 includes fraternity and sorority houses and the residence houses and hotels of other organizations. The data in the table overstate the importance of tax-exempt firms since they may actually compete with portions of the for-profit rental housing market and with for-profit hotels and motels.

[7] Excludes schools operated by religious organizations.

TABLE IV
Sectoral composition, by industry

Industry	Measurement basis	NP Share[1]	FP Share[1]	G Share[1]
Health services				
Short term and general				
hospitals	Facilities	53%	12%	35%
	Beds	62%	8%	30%
	Expenditures	65%	7%	27%
	Employment	66%	6%	28%
Psychiatric hospitals	Facilities	18%	26%	56%
Chronic care hospitals	Facilities	29%	7%	64%
Homes for mentally				
handicapped	Facilities	38%	46%	16%
Nursing homes	Facilities	34%	61%	5%
	Beds	20%	69%	11%
	Employment	24%	76%	N.A.
Education				
Elementary and secondary	Enrollment	10%	1%	89%
Secondary	Revenues	14%	3%	83%
Post-secondary	Revenues	20%	33%	47%
Higher education	Enrollment	24%	N.A.	76%
Social services				
Day care centers	Facilities	41%	52%	7%
	Enrollment	63%	27%	N.A.
	Employment	56%	44%	N.A.
Individual and family				
services	Employment	96%	4%	N.A.
Legal services	Employment	2%	98%	N.A.
Culture and entertainment				
Theater, orchestra, and				
other performing arts	Employment	26%	74%	N.A.
Radio and television				
broadcasting	Employment	5%	95%	N.A.
Art museums	Revenue	65%	5%	30%
Research				
Research and development	Expenditures	15%	72%	13%
Basic research	Expenditures	67%	18%	15%

[1] Where government share is not available, nonprofit and for-profit figures are shares of private sector activity. When for-profit share is not available separately, private sector share is reported in the nonprofit column.

Reproduced from R. Steinberg, "Nonprofit Organizations and the Market" manuscript prepared for W. Powell, ed., *Between the Public and the Private: The Not-For Profit Sector,* Yale University Press, 1986. Steinberg provides detailed information on sources in footnotes to the original table.

tures, those financed by public subsidies, are often included with "government expenditures." Nor do we have accurate records on voluntary contributions; tax returns, which are an important data source in the U.S., are not very useful in those countries where donations are not tax deductible or income taxes are not paid. Nevertheless, some fragmentary data are available. Jones (1983, p. 10) compiled data on British charities from several studies. The estimates vary but they indicate that if fees are included, government grants are under ten percent of total revenues. This data, however, should be understood in the context of the high level of direct government provision of health care and social services in Great Britain; voluntary charities are a very small part of the total.

Illustrative data have also been compiled by James (1982b) for the two polar cases of Holland and Sweden and are summarized in Table V. The nonprofit sector plays a much larger role in the Dutch than in the American economy, while the opposite is true in Sweden. For example, in Holland expenditures for NPO production are more than half the expenditures for direct government production, while in Sweden this figure is only 3%, miniscule by comparison. However, in both cases education is the key activity of NPO's and many of the same service categories in Tables I and II reappear. Private philanthropy is not very important in either country and most nonprofit funds come from the government. Also, in both countries NPO's tend to compete with the government, and not with profit-making firms.

Along similar lines, a 1981 survey of all nonprofit associations and foundations in Japan, presented in Table VI, showed that the largest number are in the field of "education and culture" and many others are related to "health, welfare and environmental issues." For Sri Lanka, Table VII gives the results of a sample survey of "charitable organizations" (conducted by James, 1982a) among which education, health, social service and religious activities again predominate. Major funding sources are international (Western) NPO's and government; private domestic philanthropy is small by comparison.

Thus, the data suggest that different countries make very different choices about the size of their nonprofit sectors, but those organizations that do exist are engaged in similar types of activities throughout the world. Many of these activities are "quasi-public

TABLE V
Total expenditures by government and NPO's

Activity	Sources of expenditure (%)		Sources of NPO revenues (%)		Share of total NPO exp.
	Direct gov't. prod.	NPO prod.	Gov't. & compulsory ins.	Private rev.*	
A. Holland, 1978					
Education[a]	39%	61%	93%	7%	37%
Culture and recreation[c]	49%	51%	85%	15%[f]	7%
Health[b]	18%	82%	84%	16%	32%
Social service and old age homes[d,e]	24%	76%	98%	2%	15%
Religion[g]	—	100%	3%	97%	2
Other (nonprofit & gov't. areas)[h]	96%	4%	81%[i]	19%[j]	7
Total	65%	35%	88%	12%	100%
B. Sweden[k], 1979					
Education[l]	94%	6%	75%	25%	35%
Culture and recreation[m,n]	70%	30%	67%	33%	37%
Health	100%	—	—	—	—
Social service and old age homes	100%	—	—	—	—
Religion[p,q]	77%	23%	4%	96%	14%
Other (nonprofit & gov't. areas)	99%	1%	100%	0%	14%
Total	97%	3%	65%	35%	100%

Source: Compiled from James 1982b, pp. 53–54, 61–63. Details of data derivation are given in that source and below.

* Most of the private revenues were derived from fees, except for religion where contributions are important.

[a] Derived from *Pocketbook of Educational Statistics*, Central Bureau of Statistics, The Hague, 1981, p. 86. It was assumed that local expenditures were divided between public and private schools in the same proportion as total expenditures and that 1/3 of university expenditures were in the private sector (both of these assumptions are consistent with the public–private division of enrollments). Private sources of funds to private schools are not officially available. On the basis of discussions with informed consultants I estimated these to be an average of 500 guilders per student for 2 million students, a total of 1 billion guilders. The actual figures are lower at the primary level, higher at the vocational and university levels. Public schools are not permitted to charge fees during the years of compulsory schooling, ages 6–16.

[b] Derived from *Kosten en financiering van de gezondheidzorg in nederland*, Ministry of Health, The Hague, 1978, pp. 42–44. This gave sources of revenue to all health institutions. To obtain the share accruing to private health institutions, these totals were multiplied by 0.82—the proportion of total patient days spent in private rather than public hospitals, according to *Health Statistics in Netherlands*, Central Bureau of Statistics, The Hague, 1979, p. 374.

[c] Derived from *Statistiek inkomsten en uitgaven van de overheid voor cultuur en recreatie*, Central Bureau of Statistics, The Hague, 1976, pp. 45, 51, 53. This gave the 1976 breakdowns of government expenditures to public and private cultural and recreational institutions. To obtain 1978 figures 1976 data were multiplied by 1.25, taking account of the increase in government expenditures on culture, recreation and social work between these two years, according to *The Netherlands Budget Memorandum*, Ministry of Finance, The Hague, 1981, p. 112.

[d] Data on social services were derived from *Statistiek inkomsten en uitgaven van de overheid voor maatschappelijk welzijn*, Central Bureau of Statistics, The Hague, 1976, pp. 43, 51, 61. This gave the 1976 breakdowns of government expenditures to public and private social service organizations. To obtain 1978 figures 1976 data were multiplied by 1.25, taking account of the increase in government expenditures on culture, recreation and social work between these two years, according to *The Netherlands Budget Memorandum, Ibid*.

[e] Data on old age homes were derived from *Statistiek van de bejaardenoorden*, Central Bureau of Statistics, The Hague, 1977, pp. 14, 54, 55. The 1977 figures given there were increased by 15% to get an approximation for 1978.

[f] Data on contributions, fees, and other private sources of income to nonprofit organizations are generally not available. This estimate is based on the fact that state and local governments derived approximately 15% of their expenditures on culture and recreation from various rents, charges, and donations according to *Statistiek van de Uitgaven der Overheid voor cultuur en recreatie*, Central Bureau of Statistics, The Hague, 1974, pp. 10–55.

[g] Derived from *Financiele gegevens kerkgenooschappen*, Central Bureau of Statistics, The Hague, 1970–76, p. 18. Data given for 1976 was increased by 15%, the rate at which church revenues increased from 1972–74 and 1974–76, to arrive at an estimate for 1978.

footnotes to table V contd.

[h] See *The Netherlands Budget Memorandum, op. cit.,* p. 21, which gives total spending of public funds by central government, local government and NPO's, combined, a total of 96.5 billion guilders.

[i] Derived from *Statistiek der rijksfinancien,* Central Bureau of Statistics, The Hague, 1971–77, pp. 25, 48, 50, 51. Data given for 1977 was increased by 15%, to take account of increases in government expenditures between 1977 and 1978.

[j] These are voluntary contributions, as reported in *Distribution of Personal Income, Part II,* Central Bureau of Statistics, The Hague, 1975, p. 205. Some of these contributions went for education, culture, health, or social service, not "other"; the breakdown across categories was not available. Since this information came from tax forms, it omits small gifts, i.e., those which are less than 1% of gross income and therefore not tax-deductible. Thus, the number given understates total donations. Many of the smaller contributions, however, went to churches and were therefore already counted as part of church finance. To the extent that some of these large contributions also went to churches, we have some double-counting which (partially) offsets the omission of small contributions. Data given for 1975 was increased by 25% to arrive at estimate for 1978.

[k] Data on central government subsidies to NPO's, direct expenditures by central government and central government transfers to local communities was assembled from material provided by the Rijksrevisionsverke (National Audit Bureau), particularly *Budget redovisning för* 1979–80, which lists each appropriation in the 1979–80 budget; a computer printout which assigns to each appropriation a purpose and type of recipient; *Statistiska meddelanden,* 1981:7, pp. 36–7, which groups all state expenditures by major purpose and type of recipient; and *Fördelningen av driftbudgetens utgifter efter ändamal,* 1981, which groups all state expenditures by major and minor purposes and type of recipient. The nonprofit sector was defined to include "associations" and "other official institutions." Data on direct local expenditures were taken from *Kommunernas Finanser* 1979, Statistiska Centralybyran, Stockholm, 1981, pp. 16, 56, 57, 59, 64, 66, 90, 94, 95.

[l] Numbers for local subsidies and private sources of income for education are based on annual financial reports of adult education associations and interviews with their officials, both of which indicated that about 25% of their revenues came from local governments, 25% from participant fees, sales of materials, interest and rent. Adult education is by far the largest NPO activity in the education category. Private primary and secondary schools probably get a higher proportion of their revenues from tuition fees and a lower proportion from municipalities, while the opposite is true for folk high schools.

[m] Local subsidies to cultural NPO's were derived from *Kulturstatistik,* published by Statens kulturrad och Statistiska centralbyran, Stockholm, 1981, p. 107. Private revenues of cultural NPO's are my estimate, based on budgetary data for cultural organizations in *Kulturstatistik, op. cit.,* p. 123 and in *Utbildningsdepartementet,*

Statsliggaren, 1980–81 (containing line-by-line expenditures for the Education Department), which suggested that private sources account for approximately 10% of total revenues for cultural institutions.

[n] Local subsidies to recreational NPO's were derived from *Fritidspolitik and Samhällstod*, National Youth Board, Stockholm, 1981, p. 76. This was confirmed by an interview with an official of the National Sports Federation. Lotteries are a major source of private funding; membership dues and admission fees are secondary sources.

[p] Approximately 75% of expenditures on religion was derived from the "parish tax," collected by local government for the Church of Sweden. Since this is a state church financed by a special church tax determined by each parish, it is considered part of the local government sector rather than the NPO sector in this table. The Free Churches are treated as NPO's, but data on local government contributions to them was not available.

[q] Data on private revenues for Swedish Free Churches are my estimate, based on the following information: According to interviews with church officials and perusal of their annual reports, there are approximately 300,000 Free Church members in Sweden, each of whom contributes an average of 3000 kroner. Also, the Svenska Missionforbundet, the largest Free Church organization in Sweden, had an income of 186 million kroner and approximately 20% of the Free Church membership and finances in the country. Both of these methods yield a total private revenue to the churches of 900–930 million kroner, from which the percentages in this table were derived.

TABLE VI
Major activities of NPO's in Japan, 1981
Percentage breakdown by numbers of organizations

Education and culture	33%
Health, welfare, environment	33%
Aid to private industry (trade assoc.)	26%
Quasi-government	8%
Total	100%

Source: Tanaka and Amemiya 1983, pp. 26, 30.

TABLE VII
Major activities of approved charities in Sri Lanka,
1979
Percentage breakdown by numbers of
organizations

Education	35%
Health and family planning	14%
Homes for orphans and elderly	14%
Sports, recreation and environment	10%
Aid to needy and emergency relief	34%
Religion	34%
Other	6%
Total	147%*

* Total is more than 100% because 2 activities
were counted for many organizations.
Source: James 1982a.

goods," such as education and health care, that yield a combination
of private and external benefits. They also tend to be labor-
intensive, human capital-enhancing services. From an international
viewpoint, competition with the public sector is more pervasive than
competition with the profit-maximizing sector. Private philanthropy
provides a unique source of NPO funding worldwide, but once we
leave the U.S., voluntary contributions are generally quite unim-
portant and government financing much more important, especially
in large nonprofit sectors. We turn now to consider the major
explanations, both normative and positive, for these universal
characteristics of nonprofit organizations.

3. THEORIES OF NPO FORMATION

What is the economic rationale for the development of the nonprofit organization? Under what circumstances can nonprofit firms coexist with or dominate for-profit and government provision of goods and services? This section presents a summary and critique of the major theories that deal with these issues. (See Hansmann, 1986 and Rose-Ackerman, 1986 for other summaries.) We set forth three normative theories which attempt to rationalize the existence of nonprofits. These theories are predicated on a series of rather idealized conceptions of the behavior of organizations facing a nondistribution constraint. Therefore, in Parts IV and V we go on to re-examine the theoretical predictions in the light of positive and empirical analyses of NPO behavior.

It is not difficult to explain the existence of zero-profit firms. In long run competitive equilibrium all firms are zero-profit. The nonprofit enterprise, in contrast, may earn positive profits; it simply has no owners to whom these profits can be distributed. Instead, all revenues must be spent within the organization. This nondistribution condition, taken on as a voluntary, publicly announced constraint, is the hallmark of the NPO. We underline the words "voluntary" and "publicly announced" because other organizational forms have similar constraints which are not voluntary or public. For example, public bureaucracies are required to return excess funds to the Treasury and the regulated utility faces a constraint on profit rates that is imposed upon it. The Baumol "sales-maximizing firm" and the Williamson firm with expense preference may operate subject to a (minimum) profit constraint which is not publicly announced or even acknowledged. As we shall see in Parts VI and VII, although each of these organizational types has a different raison d'etre, the behavioral consequences are in some respects similar to the NPO.

The first group of theories (e.g., Hansmann, 1980, 1986, Fama and Jensen, 1983a, 1983b, Thompson, 1980, Easley and O'Hara, 1983, 1986, Krashinsky, 1986, Nelson and Krashinsky, 1973) explain the line between nonprofit (NPO) and profit-maximizing (PMO) organizations by emphasizing the impact of "asymmetric information," "contract failure," and "principal-agent problems" on organizational form. The nonprofit form is said to be more "trustworthy" and hence to have greater consumer and donor appeal, when monitoring is not possible, and in some cases this trustworthiness outweighs the difficulties in raising capital and maintaining productive efficiency that arise when owner/managers are not residual claimants. Closely related to theories which emphasize trust are those theories (Ben-Ner, 1986a, 1986b) which see nonprofits as a mechanism for consumer control when other methods of monitoring are ineffective.

The second class of theories (e.g. Weisbrod, 1977, 1980) analyzes the line between nonprofit and government provision. Nonprofit provision occurs when some people are dissatisfied with the amount or variety of services provided by the government. Preston (1984a) has developed a variant of this model in which non-profits in a monopolistically competitive industry attract private donations by concentrating on those product types that generate external benefits. These firms coexist with for-profits producing purely private product qualities.

These two theories may be combined: Weisbrod's shows how the private sector may come to provide "public" goods while "contract failure" implies that, under certain circumstances, the private provision will take place in nonprofit rather than for-profit enterprises. In both cases, the nonprofit form satisfies consumer and/or donor demand better than pure profit-maximizing or governmental forms.

A third theory deals only with government decisions to funnel grant and subsidy money to nonprofits rather than to public agencies or for-profits. According to James (1986), constraints on the government's ability to use market-clearing prices and wages make it cheaper to delegate production of quasi-public goods to the private sector and monitoring problems frequently make it politically expedient to choose nonprofit rather than for-profit organizations for this delegation and subsidy.

A. Nonprofits vs. for-profits: contract failure and asymmetric information

1. *Unobservable quantity or quality.*   In simple competitive models the profit-maximizing firm, with its single-minded pursuit of private gain, makes decisions that are optimal for society as a whole. The

efficiently operating PMO is thus viewed as the benchmark organizational form. However, it is widely recognized by economists that PMO's will not produce efficient outcomes under all conditions. In particular, when information is asymmetric, when output is unobservable or when principal-agent problems exist, profit-maximization can lead to inefficient outcomes and alternative organizational arrangements may be superior. We examine how NPO's, operating under a nondistribution constraint, can be organized as a response to these difficulties.

Henry Hansmann (1980, 1986) provides the fullest development of the asymmetric information argument and Easley and O'Hara (1983, 1986) have developed a more general formulation. In Hansmann's model, the producer has more information about product quality than the consumer does. Since consumers cannot observe certain quality characteristics, they are unable to monitor them and producers will always have an incentive to cheat. Hence, contracts for these characteristics will not be written or enforced and they will be underproduced and underconsumed in ordinary profit-maximizing markets (Akerlof 1970). The nondistribution constraint allegedly reduces the incentive for the firm to downgrade quality and reassures the consumer that high quality will be maintained. The consumer, finding the nonprofit firm more "trustworthy," is willing to contract with it for goods whose quality cannot be monitored. NPO's have a comparative advantage in the provision of such goods, and enhance the overall efficiency of the marketplace by enabling them to be produced and consumed. Typically, these "commercial nonprofits" depend on fees for service and share the market with for-profits, the former supposedly guaranteeing quality, the latter offering greater productive efficiency. (A similar justification for the existence of "donative nonprofits" will be discussed below).

Easley and O'Hara deal with a situation in which output (quantity or quality) and managerial effort are not observable but inputs are. The PMO, in such a situation, will not produce any output nor will the manager expend any effort; instead, he will simply capture for personal gain any fees paid by prospective consumers. Obviously, consumers will be unwilling to enter into such contracts. Easley and O'Hara define the nonprofit firm as one in which the manager is required to expend at least a minimum observable level of effort and the remuneration to the manager is fixed so that the remainder of the purchase price must be devoted to other costs of production. This nonprofit contract may indeed produce output and be viable in the sense that producers and consumers are willing to enter into it. Note, however, that the nonprofit contract "works" only if one can verify that the manager has put forth some effort and has hired productive factors with his revenues. Otherwise, shirking and waste may dominate, making the nonprofit form no more viable than the for-profit. One response to this problem, suggested by Hansmann (1985) is to have the state police nonprofits to reduce shirking. But this makes the determination of optimal organizational form turn, not on market forces, but on government behavior. Is managerial shirking in NPO's more easily monitored by public agencies than is managerial remuneration in PMO's? Are nonprofits trusted because they are more likely to be effectively regulated, or because of their voluntary nondistribution constraint? In fact, neither NPO's nor PMO's are monitored much by the government, so, as discussed at length in Part IV, the potential for shirking remains.

According to the "contract failure" models of Hansmann and Easley and O'Hara, the "quality" of goods in which "commercial NPO's" specialize ought to be more difficult to evaluate than that of goods produced by ordinary PMO's. In theory, this is one testable implication of these models, which should allow us to judge their validity. Unfortunately, we have no objective way to quantify this informational asymmetry, nor is the impressionistic evidence clear-cut. While it may be difficult to shop around for and acquire information about nursing homes and child day-care centers, and to transfer from one to another, all three institutional forms (NPO, PMO and government) seem able to co-exist in these industries for long periods of time. In contrast, detailed information is available about the selectivity, student/faculty ratios, faculty credentials and alumni of colleges and universities, where the nonprofit form dominates in the private sector. Many people feel they can directly evaluate the quality of ballet or opera companies, and it does not seem likely that the legal status of the organization (often public or nonprofit) enters into their evaluation. Some people have a "trusting" relationship with their doctors or lawyers, who are certainly not "nonprofit." Thus, it is not clear on a priori grounds that the quality (or other output characteristics) of nonprofit services is more difficult to evaluate than the quality of, say, used cars, which are sold exclusively by profit-maximizers, or that nonprofits are uniformly "trusted" more than for-profits. In fact, the one piece of empirical evidence we have, a telephone survey conducted by Permut (1981), indicates that people often do not even know which organizations are nonprofit and which are for-profit. Nevertheless, if at least some people believe that the nonprofit label signifies high quality, commercial nonprofits may be able to establish a market niche in spite of competition from PMOs. In Part IV we present behavioral models of NPO's which throw further light on these issues.

2. *Customer control.*   Direct control by customers may be desired to assure high quality (e.g. in a day care center where parents want to control the way it is run) or may be a way to shift profits to consumers (e.g. in natural monopolies) (see Hansmann 1980.) Consumer cooperatives are one institutional mechanism for accomplishing this; they are the equivalent of a "for-profit" enterprise where consumers, rather than stockholders, receive the profits. A mutual nonprofit, run by consumers, is another institutional mechanism; here the nondistribution constraint holds and all profits must be retained in the organization (cf. McGuire, 1972). In both cases, a problem arises because of the need to monitor the day-to-day manager, whose interest may diverge from those of the "consumer-owners" (just as they may from those of stockholder-owners—the familiar separation of ownership from control problem).

When will the nonprofit rather than the for-profit form be used as a mechanism for achieving consumer control? It would appear that, when the rationale for consumer control is mainly monetary, the for-profit (consumer cooperative) form would dominate, since the nonprofit form adds a nonessential constraint. In contrast, when the strongest objective is to maintain high quality, the nonprofit form, which reinvests all earnings, might be preferable. This is consistent with the model developed by Ben-Ner (1986a, 1986b), where consumer control reduces managerial tendencies to misrepresent and underproduce quality.

It is also consistent with the widespread use of volunteer labor by NPO's, particularly in the social services, and the presence of large donor-consumers on the boards of directors of opera companies, museums, and universities. Both the volunteer workers and the directors serve to monitor the output characteristics of the organization. Explicit consumer control over quality, in some cases, merely reinforces the implicit insurance which is supposedly provided by the nonprofit institutional form. It suggests that consumers are aware that the nondistribution constraint, by itself, does not always do the job (cf. Fama and Jensen 1983a, 1983b).

3. *Principal-agent problems and private philanthropy.* Theories which focus on potential donations as a raison d'etre for the development of NPO's are closely related to theories stressing unobservable quality. In Hansmann's model (1980), the donor is a customer who wishes to increase the organization's quantity or quality; but, since he does not receive a product as his quid pro quo he cannot directly observe the marginal impact of his gift. Again, asymmetric information leads to contract failure (unwillingness of potential donors to donate) in profit-maximizing markets. The "nondistribution of the residual" constraint, again, is said to increase the "trustworthiness" of the organization and hence, encourage donations. Thus, "donative NPO's" would be found in areas where the potential for private contributions exists. These donations may be gifts of money or time (volunteer labor). Fama and Jensen (1983a, 1983b) present the same argument in principal-agent terms: the donor is the principal, the organization's manager is the agent, and the nondistribution constraint is a control mechanism designed to rule out gross misappropriation and increase the likelihood that the agent will act in accordance with the principal's wishes.

In Part IV, on NPO behavior, we investigate in some detail whether the nondistribution constraint, in fact, produces this result. We show there that, while the NPO manager cannot directly capture the profit or donation, he may do so in many disguised forms. For example, he may divert excessive revenues to staff and emoluments (just as Williamson's firm with expense preference would); he may put forth little effort to reduce x-inefficiency (Leibenstein 1966) or shirking (Alchian and Demsetz 1971); and, in a multi-product NPO he may downgrade the quality of one good in order to cross-subsidize another which he prefers (James 1983,

James and Neuberger 1981), Thus, on theoretical grounds, it appears that a customer or donor who places his blind trust in the security provided by the nondistribution constraint may be misled.

What do the facts show? Are people more likely to donate to NPO's? Consistent with the theory just summarized, in the American nonprofit sector as a whole, about 25% of all revenues do indeed come from private philanthropy (Tables I and II), while people rarely if ever contribute to PMO's. Industries dominated by PMO's do not depend on voluntary contributions. However, as these tables also show, nonprofits exist in many industries (e.g. health care) where donations play a relatively small role, and if we were to break this data down by firm we would find many individual NPO's that operate without donations even in "high philanthropic" industries (e.g. education). Furthermore, private philanthropy is much less important in most other countries, including some with large nonprofit sectors (Tables V and VI). Thus, the evidence suggests that NPO's have a comparative advantage over PMO's where potential donations exist, but this is not a necessary condition for NPO survival and dominance.

If NPO's are found in industries where potential donations exist, this leads one to ask why people donate for certain goods but not for others. Donations are a puzzle to economists because they appear to contradict the free rider behavior which stems from the utility functions ordinarily assumed. If people care only about their own consumption, they will rarely make donations where there is no direct, material quid pro quo. It has been shown that if people care about the consumption or utility of others (Collard, 1978; Daly and Giertz, 1977; Danielsen, 1975; Hochman and Rodgers, 1969, 1973; Pigou, 1948, pp. 710–712), or if they believe the charity will ultimately rebound to their own benefit (Becker, 1976; Hirshleifer, 1978; Tullock, 1971), they may be willing to donate. However, mere feelings of concern for others are not sufficient to generate donations. People can "feel good" about the benefits provided to the poor without spending any of their own resources if other people make contributions (Sugden, 1984). Furthermore, as Wintrobe (1981, 1983) points out, Becker's and Hirshleifer's models require that a set of very restrictive conditions be satisfied and are not applicable to impersonal, large-number situations.

These free rider problems may be overcome if people desire a personal connection between their own gifts and the charitable services provided by a nonprofit. Rose-Ackerman (1982) has suggested, for example, that a kind of "buying-in" mentality may exist under which people do not believe it is appropriate to "feel good" about a charity's activities unless they have personally contributed to the organization (see also Arrow, 1974). In a related analysis Sugden (1984) argues that many people subscribe to a principle of reciprocity under which they believe they have an obligation to contribute at least as much as everyone else to provide a public good that benefits everyone. Collard (1978) proposes a "contagion" theory under which the altruism of some people stimulates the altruism of others. In addition to these personal moral principles, informal social pressures may be exerted on people to convince them to contribute "voluntary taxes" to their communities. Sometimes the donors are repaid with status and prestige if they contribute substantially (Pigou, 1948, pp. 713–714) or social ostracism if they do not contribute at all (Ireland and Johnson, 1970; Keating, Pitts and Appel, 1981; and Long, 1976, provide some empirical evidence of this phenomenon). More subtly, people may be "socialized" to behave unselfishly, consistent with social rather than individual welfare (cf. Margolis, 1982; Phelps, ed., 1975; Titmus, 1971; Tullock, 1966).

This discussion suggests that, while a substantial tendency to free-ride remains, some of it has been overcome, and donations will be found where large groups in society desire goods characterized by external benefits or decreasing costs or where income redistribution is the objective. These are, of course, the classical arguments for government action, and tax revenues presently provide the bulk of financial support for programs designed to further these goals. But it should be recalled that voluntary "nonprofit" social mechanisms existed long before strong governments did—and some of these mechanisms still survive. In this sense, government and philanthropic nonprofits are alternative responses to the same problem; if NPO's prevail over PMO's where donations exist, they will, at the same time, be found in areas (such as health, education, social service and culture) where government is a potential or actual competitor. We move on then, to theories which analyze the division of responsibility between government and the private nonprofit sector.

B. The nonprofit sector as a producer of public goods: excess demand, heterogeneous demand and decreasing costs

Weisbrod (1977) was the first scholar to develop a model in which nonprofit organizations are characterized as producers of public goods. In Weisbrod's work, nonprofits are a response to government failure, rather than market failure. Government production of public goods is determined by some collective choice mechanism such as majority voting, but a Lindahl tax system for one reason or another is impossible to implement. Thus, since marginal tax prices differ from marginal benefits, some people will prefer larger amounts of the public good. If the summation of their benefits from a marginal unit exceeds the cost of producing it, additional provision may take place through the private sector. If government production does not go down as a result and if private benefits do not exceed social benefits, the possibility of supplementary private production moves us closer to efficiency. While his first model focused on diverse tastes regarding *quantity,* Weisbrod later extended it to cover diverse tastes regarding the *type* of public good in situations where the government-produced output is standardized. The private sector then provides more product variety.

It is possible that, once privately-produced public goods are available, people will vote for less government production. Then, the total amount produced may go down, not up (Weiss, 1986). Weisbrod models the private sector as responding to the government, but not vice versa. In the real world, a system of simultaneous determination may be more appropriate (Roberts, 1984; Seaman, 1979; Weiss, 1986). In any event, the positive implications remain: once any decision about government production of public goods has been made, some people may decide to supplement it through the private sector.

Cursory examination of the nonprofit sector does indeed appear consistent with the Weisbrod hypothesis. Health, education and social services are often said to have some "public good" characteristics, although they are hardly pure public goods and the alleged externalities are difficult to measure. A state-by-state cross-sectional analysis by Lee and Weisbrod (1977) which sought to explain the share of nonprofit versus government hospitals as a function of various indicators of heterogeneous taste, produced somewhat supportive results. In analyzing redistribution through government action versus donations to non-profits, Feigenbaum (1980) also finds that philanthropy is relatively greater in more heterogeneous communities. James (1984) and James and Benjamin (1984) present evidence that the private educational sectors in Japan and Holland are due to excess demand and differentiated demand, respectively. Levy (1986) points to both motives in explaining the growth of private higher education in Latin America and Geiger (1984) does so for other countries. More generally, excess demand-driven private sectors are found primarily in developing countries, while heterogeneous tastes seem to be the principal force in modern industrial societies.

The Weisbrod model explains why private provision of public goods may exist. However, it does not explain why this private production is nonprofit. Our preceding discussion throws some light on this issue. If people are willing to donate to goods with "public" characteristics, then NPO's will have a comparative advantage over PMO's in capturing these donations, so the most effective private producer of "public" goods will be the nonprofit firm (Preston, 1984a). In a sense, the nonprofit sector is defined by the intersection of market failure and government failure, with NPO's producing goods with some "public" characteristics.

The nonprofit form may also permit private provision of goods that have high fixed costs, low marginal costs, and benefits that vary widely across people. How can we cover the costs of producing such goods, in cases where total benefits exceed total cost but there is no uniform price for which total revenue exceeds costs? These are "public goods" for which government provision is one classic answer. Private provision with price discrimination is another possibility, but if there is no way to identify "high benefit" and "low benefit" people a priori, price discrimination is difficult to impose. Voluntary price discrimination through donations may be a viable alternative if the free rider problem can be overcome, as when people are members of a relatively small consumer group and derive a large consumer surplus. Then they may be willing to contribute and, for the reasons given above, they may prefer to contribute to nonprofits rather than for-profits. Hansmann (1981) develops this point of view as an explanation for the importance of non-profits in the arts, e.g. opera companies, symphony orchestras and museums.

Consistent with the above analysis, we might expect "donative nonprofits," i.e., those heavily dependent on voluntary contributions, to be producers of goods with large "public" components, while "commercial nonprofits," which rely on product sales, to have some other raison d'etre. Weisbrod (1980) has calculated a "collectiveness index" which measures the share of total revenues derived from gifts and donations in various nonprofit industries and argues that there is an apparent correlation between this index and the degree of "publicness" of the serivce in question. However, since we do not have an objective way of measuring the latter, the evidence for such a correlation is only impressionistic at this point.

C. Public subsidies as a reason for nonprofit production

Private philanthropy is characteristic of the American nonprofit sector, much less common abroad. However, government subsidies to nonprofits are important almost everywhere. (See Tables I and II for data on the U.S., Table V for data on Holland and Sweden.) Thus, it is unclear whether, market forces or political forces lie behind the formation of NPO's, since large nonprofit sectors are rarely found without substantial government grants. Even in the U.S., "public" philanthropy exceeds private philanthropy if implicit tax subsidies are included. An empirical study by Hansmann using state-by-state cross-sectional data for hospitals, nursing homes, primary, secondary and vocational education indicates that favorable property and income tax treatment significantly enhances the market share of nonprofit organizations (1985 and 1982). Frech and Ginsburg (1978, 1980) and Vogel (1977) show how tax subsidies benefit nonprofit health insurers.

Drawing on these empirical observations, James (1986) argues that nonprofits flourish precisely in those areas where government has accepted some financing responsibility but has chosen to delegate production to NPO's rather than in areas chosen by decentralized consumers or private donors. While most of the following discussion concerns explicit delegation and subsidy, the same principles apply where the delegation is implicit but differentially favors some industries and locations over others. The arguments given below are examined in greater detail, from a normative and empirical viewpoint, in Part VIII.

Why, then, does the government sometimes delegate production of public and quasi-public goods rather than producing itself, and when does it delegate to nonprofit rather than for-profit enterprises? First of all, private organizations may be better able to charge fees for services, so that the government's share of total cost is reduced when production responsibility is delegated to them. For example, private schools in many countries charge tuition which covers part of their costs. This would lead us to expect such delegation to occur for quasi-public goods, which yield some divisible private benefits, rather than for nonexcludable public goods. This hypothesis seems consistent with the facts.

Second, private organizations also may face lower costs than government institutions, especially for labor. James (1986) points to numerous cases in which the public sector is required by law to pay wages which are above market-clearing levels, while the private sector is free to hire equivalent services at lower cost. "Contracting out" is one way for the government to evade these constraints. If politicians face pressure to provide more public services, and also face resistance to higher taxes, subsidies to private producers enable them to increase output at lower taxpayer costs. Even highly paid civil servants are unlikely to protest so long as their own jobs and salaries are insulated from declines in public production. (Conversely, private firms may be able to pay *higher* salaries than the public sector to specialized personnel, such as research scientists, and may therefore be able to attract higher quality people to work on projects desired by government.)

Finally, in some instances policymakers may prefer to provide services differentiated by language, religion, etc., but government may be bureaucratically unable to supply such a wide range of services itself. In such cases, subsidization of private organizations is a logical development.

But why should the government choose NPO's rather than PMO's as the recipients of its largesse? Sometimes, of course, it does not. For example, large defense contracts are administered by private firms, local governments commonly contract with for-profit trash haulers, and recently PMO's have even begun providing prison service. Nevertheless, there are reasons for governments to prefer NPO's in some circumstances. In the case just discussed, the relevant private organizations (e.g. religious) may only exist as

NPO's. Furthermore, where the potential for donations of volunteer time or money exists, NPO's may be able to provide more matching resources than PMO's and hence would be preferred by the government.

In addition, in industries characterized by many small enterprises, providing intangible services rather than countable objects, monitoring by the government would be very costly. The one-way term "subsidy" or "grant" rather than the reciprocal term "purchase" or "contract" is used precisely in such cases, where the quid pro quo is difficult to measure. Nonprofit status of the recipient may then reassure the government and substitute for monitoring; at least, the subsidies will not be distributed by NPO's as pecuniary profits. Politicians may have a high preference for avoiding scandal, and subsidies to NPO's may be considered "safer" than payments to PMO's in industries where output cannot be readily observed. In contrast, concentrated industries with a small number of large firms which can more easily be monitored or regulated (e.g. defense, space) the government deals with PMO's. However, even these contracts are often written on a cost-plus basis, in effect turning part of the PMO into a constrained-profit enterprise for purposes of dealing with the government.

Thus, asymmetric information and the principal-agent problem reappear as an explanation for NPO survival even in societies where private donations are small. NPO's exist, however, not because of the independent choices of many small donors, but, rather, because one large donor with power to set basic contractual terms—the government—is seeking a method for providing quasi-public goods which will involve the least political cost.

4. MODELS OF NPO BEHAVIOR: COMPARISON WITH PMO'S

The previous section dealt with idealized theories of NPO formation, in which the demand for nonprofit provision arose from various types of market and planning failure. While government and profit-maximizing enterprises behaved in nonoptimal ways, nonprofits were believed immune to some of these negative incentives and constraints. In reviewing these theories, we raised questions about whether this was a correct expectation about nonprofit behavior. We now present several models of NPO behavior and related empirical evidence in order to examine this question more systematically. (For another discussion of some of these models see Steinberg, 1986a.) These models contrast NPO and PMO behavior under the assumption that NPO managers maximize their own utility in much the same way that PMO managers in competitive markets maximize profits. Here, profit-maximizing competitive behaviour is taken as the efficient norm. Thus, while the theories presented in Part III idealized the non-profit sector, in this section we idealize the for-profit sector. After presenting a litany of non-profit "failures" in this section, we go on in Part V to develop a more balanced view.

One immediate difficulty is that we have no self-evident objective function for the NPO, as we do for the PMO or for other institutional forms such as the sales-maximizing or staff-maximizing firm. Instead, the NPO is defined by the nondistribution constraint, and we are left to speculate on what its objective might be. In that sense, NPO's are very much like consumers, who are said to maximize their utility but who have different and unspecified utility functions. NPO's differ from consumers, however, in that we cannot simply assume their existence. In order to say very much about NPO behavior, then, we must explain why people found NPO's and also put some content into the objective functions of managers. A variety of models have been developed, dealing with different industries, assuming different goals and producing correspondingly different results. Further complicating the analysis, the NPO revenue function is sometimes difficult to define, particularly where donations are involved. Finally, the possibility of x-inefficiency and shirking in the NPO makes its cost function difficult to characterize. Therefore, we begin in this section with an existing, output-maximizing NPO and compare its behavior (choice of quantity) to that of a PMO with the same cost and revenue functions. Using this model as a benchmark, we proceed to successively more complex models in which fixed donations or shirking may exist and quality, technology or product mix may enter into the managerial objective function.

A. Single product competitive NPO: output maximization

1. *The Basic Model.*   Consider a single-product NPO in which all revenues come from sales of the product (Q). The price of the

product (P) may be paid directly by the consumer, or indirectly by the government or a third-party donor. In any case, we assume there is a direct and verifiable quid pro quo for the payment, with subsidies and donations contingent upon output and hence indistinguishable from consumer payments. We also assume initially that the firm operates on its cost curve ($C(Q)$) and that price is established by supply and demand in a competitive market. We consider a very simple objective function under which the manager seeks to maximize output. This objective function would make sense if the manager's prestige or promotion possibilities are positively related to enterprise size or if he hopes to proselytize by reaching the largest possible audience. Thus, the utility of the NPO manager is $U = U(Q)$, $dU/dQ > 0$. Saving for future production is not an option in this static single-product model.

The NPO, then, maximizes $U = U(Q)$ subject to the constraint that $C(Q) = PQ$. Assuming standard short-run, U-shaped average cost and marginal cost curves, U is maximized at Q_2 in Figure 1. Thus, the single product NPO will produce more than the PMO would in the short run (Q_2 rather than Q_1). It follows that, under these simplified conditions, where PMO production is Pareto-optimal, NPO production will not be optimal, since marginal cost (MC) exceeds price.

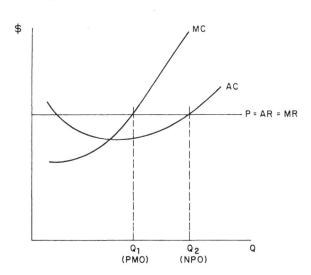

These conclusions however, do not necessarily hold in the long run. Long run equilibrium depends on conditions for the entry of new firms and the expansion of existing firms and, as we shall see below, these may be different for NPO's and PMO's. If we assume for the moment that they are the same, entry of PMO's and/or NPO's will take place so long as new entrants can at least break even. Then, price will fall to minimum AC, and the industry will have the same equilibrium P, Q, and number of firms in the long run, regardless of whether the firms are PMO's or NPO's. All the optimality (or nonoptimality) properties of the former are possessed by the latter. There seem to be no special efficiency reasons for or against the nonprofit mode of organization in this case, where revenue is tied to output, output is observable, cost functions, demand curves and entry conditions are the same, and the maximum possible profits are zero.

Not surprisingly, it is difficult to locate pure industries of this type. Closely analogous, however, are small-scale producers of day care for children, where individual reputation is critical, capital requirements are negligible, organizational form may be irrelevant, and NPO's and PMO's co-exist (cf. Rose-Ackerman, 1983).

2. *The importance of donations.* Suppose now, that public or private donations are a possible source of revenue, and that these cannot be made contingent on output. Earlier, we discussed theories of NPO formation which argued that: 1) Donors are willing to make contributions to "worthwhile" causes: e.g. outputs with positive externalities; 2) Donors typically cannot verify whether their contributions have induced additional output, hence; 3) They will prefer to donate to NPO's rather than PMO's under these circumstances. Then, NPO's will have different revenue curves from PMO's, which may in turn produce different behavior. We now investigate these points more systematically.

Donations which are not a function of output, because of monitoring difficulties, may be termed "fixed revenue" (FR) and the firm's average revenue curve becomes $AR = P + AFR$ which, as shown in Figure 2, lies above $MR = P$ if FR is positive. While the existence of a positive FR has no effect on MR or, therefore, on the short run output of the PMO, it raises the budget constraint and hence the output of the NPO (to Q_3). (For similar reasons, changes

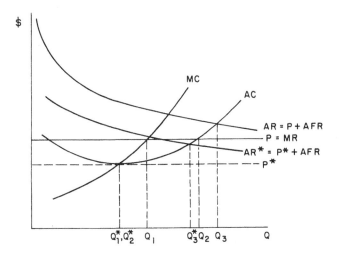

FIGURE 2   Equilibrium price and output in long run and short run with fixed donations.

in fixed costs or lump-sum taxes influence NPO output.) The NPO, like the consumer or the utility-maximizing (Baumol or Williamson) firm, but unlike the PMO, changes its behavior in response to changes in net income even if all relative prices remain the same. Thus, this behavioral model is consistent with Hansmann's and Fama and Jensen's proposition that NPO's are the preferred institutional form for donations. If NPO managers seek to maximize output, donors are correct in believing that NPO's but not PMO's will increase short run output when contributions rise, even in situations where monitoring costs make it impossible to tie donations directly to output.

Long-run equilibrium is more difficult to define once donations are introduced, since it depends on the entry of new firms and their access to donations. Suppose, first, that *FR* is positive for a small set of existing NPO's but new NPO's have little or no access to donations. This is consistent with a finding by Weisbrod and Dominguez (1986) of a positive age effect on donations, which may exist because people are more willing to contribute to (have greater confidence in) established organizations or because payroll deductions go to organizations with a known track record (e.g. for members of United Way, etc.). We assume that initially price exceeds minimum average cost. Then, new NPO's and PMO's enter, forcing down P to minimum AC (at P^*) and the two institutional forms can coexist. While the old NPO's (with donations) produce Q_3^*, more than the new NPO's (Q_2^*) or the PMO's (Q_1^*), (i.e. Q_1^* and Q_2^* both occur at the same point, where $P^* = \min. AC$, Q_3^* at a higher point where $P^* + AFR = AC^* > \min AC$), aggregate output for the industry as a whole is just sufficient to clear the market at $P^* = \min AC$ and therefore is not greater than it would have been in the absence of donations. In this sense, the donors have not achieved their objective of increasing overall output. Nor is this outcome efficient, since different organizations have different MC's, in the long run equilibrium. This result occurs, however, because only the old firms receive donations, an anomaly which the model itself does not justify, and because the initial price was greater than minimum AC.

At the opposite extreme, suppose that FR is positive for existing NPO's and new NPO's also have ready access to similar donations. New firms then enter so long as they may operate without incurring a loss. As depicted in Figure 3, the entry of new firms causes P and AR to shift downward until $P^* < \text{minimum } AC$ and AR^* is just tangential to AC for the marginal NPO. Production takes place at

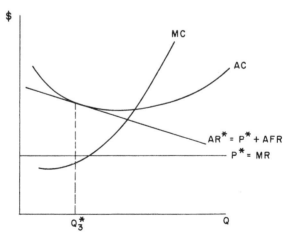

FIGURE 3   Equilibrium price and output in long run with fixed donations and free entry.

the point of tangency, regardless of the manager's utility function. Since AR^* is negatively sloped, this must occur to the left of minimum AC. Thus, if FR is positive for both old and new NPO's, P^*, the price paid by beneficiaries, is lower, implying that long run industry Q is higher, in the nonprofit than in the profit-maximizing industry. Thus, the donors have achieved their objective of increasing aggregate output. However, they have done so by sacrificing productive efficiency. There are many small NPO's, none producing at the minimum point on its AC curve, each with considerable "excess capacity" and with potential gains from merger. Needless to say, PMO's cannot exist in such a circumstance, since P^* is less than AC. Provision of social services below cost, to needy consumers, may be an example. (It is interesting to note that profit-maximizing monopolistic competition models, too, are characterized by excess capacity and potential gains from mergers. However, in that case $P = AC$ since there are no donations, hence PMO's exist, but productive inefficiency is the price paid for product variety.)

This trade-off between higher quantity and productive efficiency in the nonprofit sector is one which recurs in many of the models we present below. It appears that the greater social good is often achievable only at an efficiency cost, whether the government or the nonprofit institutional form is used to remedy the market failure of profit-maximizing firms.

3. *Are cost functions the same*? *Shirking and property rights models.* In their theory of the firm, Alchian and Demsetz (1972) view the residual claimant as a "team manager" who has the incentive to minimize shirking because he will receive the generated profit. If managers are not residual claimants, this incentive is reduced. While separation of ownership and control leads to principal-agent problems in large corporations, some would argue that the possibility of "takeovers" through the capital market serves as the ultimate threat which assures the survival of those managers who do maximize profits and minimize shirking. In the nonprofit world, however, managers are not residual claimants and there are no shares to be sold in takeovers. Hence, we would expect to find more bureaucratized control mechanisms, more shirking, and higher cost curves. Managers may overpay themselves, relative to opportunity cost, may have plush offices, hire their relatives and

discriminate against groups they dislike, on personal rather than productivity grounds.

This line of thought emphasizes the negative consequences which occur when property rights (to dividends, capital gains, transfer of ownership) are attenuated (Clarkson, 1980). It assumes that money is the best motivator, that managers will not be equally driven toward efficiency by their desire to maximize product quantity or other arguments in their objective functions. Several empirical studies have attempted to test the hypotheses stemming from the property rights models (see Steinberg 1986a). For example, Frech (1980), Frech and Ginsburg (1981), and Blair, Ginsburg and Vogel (1975) find that, in the health insurance industry, Blue Cross and Blue Shield, which are NPO's, have larger managerial emoluments, higher administrative costs, longer processing time and more errors than PMO's. After controlling for case-mix, Bays (1979) found that nonprofit hospitals are not more expensive than for-profits generally, but are significantly more expensive than for-profit chains. Clarkson (1972) found that boards of nonprofit hospitals try to control their managers by imposing more explicit rules and accounting procedures than obtain in proprietary hospitals, but greater variability in costs and input utilization remains. However, he did not control for product mix differentials. This is a significant weakness since for-profit hospitals typically specialize in more routine diagnoses than nonprofits. Feigenbaum (1983) found that medical charities in highly competitive markets spend less on administration than those in less competitive markets. Thus, there is some supportive evidence for the hypothesis that, once nonprofits are freed from competitive constraints, managers will not have the incentive to stay on the cost-minimizing frontier, but this evidence is far from conclusive.

It should be noted that, if PMO's are free to enter the industry, donations are zero, and NPO's cannot differentiate their product from PMO's, then NPO's are unable to engage in wasteful spending. Since the maximum potential profits are zero and long-run losses are ruled out, all organizations must behave exactly the same way—with maximum efficiency. Shirking is possible in the long run only if there are barriers to entry, if donations are positive for some organizations, or if some customers prefer nonprofits as more "trustworthy." Ironically, donations and trust make things worse rather than better in this respect. In effect, "shirking" is one possible use of donations and other revenues induced by trust.

The coexistence of PMO's forces productive efficiency on NPO's. However, in the simple model presented in the preceding section, the coexistence of the two forms implied that donations had failed to increase aggregate output and lower equilibrium price. We thus reiterate the trade-off between optimal amounts and optimal costs in situations where donations are a possible response to positive externalities. Put another way, in situations where a profit oriented market will not produce efficient amounts (as where externalities exist), mechanisms (such as voluntary donations) that allow increased production also allow productive inefficiency (excess capacity, shirking) and society faces a trade-off between the two kinds of inefficiency.

B. Technological preference

Nonprofit managers may not only raise costs because of shirking and excess capacity, they may also do so because of technological preference, i.e., a preference for one factor combination over another. This preference may arise because certain modes of production (e.g. the use of lavish expense accounts, plush offices, attractive secretaries) are considered more prestigious or enjoyable than others. Alternatively, it may be justified by a (correct or mistaken) belief that higher cost functions produce a higher quality product. For example, many professors advocate a small-class technology on these grounds, although the empirical evidence on this issue is far from clear. The relationship between cost and quality preference will be discussed in the next section. Here, we explore the implications of a pure technological preference.

The case of a profit-making firm which trades off some of its potential profits for the higher cost functions of a preferred technology has already been explored in the literature and will be reviewed later in this paper (see sections on Williamson's discretionary firm and the regulated utility). An NPO, denied the option of a monetary residual, is even more likely to make such a tradeoff, just as it is more likely to shirk. An important distinction must be made, however, between technological preferences that affect the marginal cost of output and hence affect the equilibrium quantity chosen, versus preferences for "perks" and emoluments which are simply funded out of "potential profits" and have no marginal impact. In the latter case, "perk" maximization is equivalent to profit maximization and the perk-maximizing NPO will behave exactly like a PMO (except that the distribution of surplus will differ).

The problems which arise in the former case can be illustrated by supposing that the NPO manager of, say, a hospital or research laboratory, prefers to use capital rather than labor, so that his $U = U[K, Q(L, K)]$. Maximizing this objective subject to a zero-profit constraint, the NPO will choose a factor mix where:

$$\frac{\partial U/\partial K + \partial U/\partial Q(\partial Q/\partial K)}{\partial U/\partial Q(\partial Q/\partial L)} = \frac{P(\partial Q/\partial K) - P_K}{P(\partial Q/\partial L) - P_L}$$

i.e. where the manager's subjective marginal rate of substitution between K and L equal, their relative net marginal cost. This contrasts with the point chosen by a PMO or by an NPO without technological preference, where:

$$\frac{\partial Q/\partial K}{\partial Q/\partial L} = \frac{P_K}{P_L}$$

i.e., where the marginal rate of technical substitution (MRTS) between K and L equals the relative factor price.

The NPO with a technological preference for capital uses an inefficiently large amount and will not be operating on its minimum cost curve. Furthermore, if the economy consists of mixtures of PMO's and NPO's with different technological preferences, each NPO will have a different MRTS, which will generally differ from that in PMO's, and society will not be operating on its production possibilities frontier. Empirical evidence does indeed indicate that technologies (L/K ratios, L/Q ratios) vary much more among NPO's than PMO's, consistent with the concept of technological preference (see James, 1983, Cohn, 1975, Balderston, 1974, O'Donoghue, 1971, for education; Clarkson, 1972, Clark, 1980, for hospitals). Lee (1971) develops a model in which non-profit hospitals acquire sophisticated equipment and highly trained personnel as "status symbols," beyond the point needed for actual production. The rapid increase in expensive hospital inputs, much of which remains underutilized, over the past two decades, is consistent with this model. The interpretation of the empirical evidence is, however, complicated by the fact that the quality and variety of output as well as technology vary across firms.

The situation is improved if there is free entry of PMO's, bringing the product price to minimum AC and making it more difficult for NPO's that operate inefficiently to survive. However, the problem is exacerbated by donations to NPO's which may be "spent" on technological preference, and by the NPO's access to factors of production at lower prices than those paid by PMO's: e.g., volunteer labor, contributed equipment, exemption from unemployment compensation and property taxes, etc. These "particularistic" factor prices lead different institutional forms to have different marginal factor productivities, again, a divergence from social efficiency. While cost subsidization can be justified if tied to all inputs engaged in producing a given class of activities (e.g. in the production of goods which yield externalities), there does not appear to be a welfare rationale for giving them only to NPO's and not to PMO's in the same industry unless the NPO's are, in fact, producing a different and more socially beneficial mix of products than PMO's.

C. Quality as a nonprofit objective

"Quality" plays an important role in several nonprofit models. NPO's are usually expected to make different quality choices from PMO's, but there is considerable controversy over which form is preferable. On the one hand, when quality is unobservable, NPO's have less incentive to cheat than PMO's, and are hence a more efficient institutional form for satisfying consumer preferences for high quality. On the other hand, NPO managers are sometimes accused of overemphasizing quality, or spending more on quality than is optimal for donors or beneficiaries. While these models disagree on welfare implications, they agree that the preferences of nonprofit managers can greatly influence the outcome, usually leading them to have more (and possibly too much) quality, which in turn means higher costs than would obtain for PMO's. The higher costs seen here are, however, attributable to quality and not to shirking, x-inefficiency or technological preference which have no corresponding benefit for donors and customers.

In the Hansmann model, discussed in Part III, consumers are

unable to make enforceable contracts with respect to characteristics that are not easily observed and measured. In areas such as health and education, product quality may be such a characteristic, and PMO's in these industries would then have a tendency to downgrade quality. NPO's, however, have less pecuniary incentive to downgrade quality. Moreover, quality may enter directly into the objective function of the NPO manager, who may be selected or self-selected into NPO management partly for this reason. Such organizations would then provide higher quality service than PMO's and would be preferred by consumers because of this expectation.

The higher quality may be financed by donations or fees. If by fees, price differentials among NPO's (which are observable) may be taken as an indicator of quality differentials (which are not), and people who are willing to pay the higher cost needed for higher quality do so. This sorts people efficiently, those with a high preference for quality purchasing from high quality institutions and vice versa. It also means that in the nonprofit as in the for-profit sector, people with higher incomes will be better able to consume higher quality.

If the higher quality is financed by donations rather than fees, this automatic sorting mechanism (by taste and income) fails. Instead, fees may be the same in high quality institutions, which receive large donations, and low quality institutions, which do not, there will be an excess demand for the former, and some kind of non-price rationing mechanism must be used. In American higher education, for example, institutions with a reputation for "quality" tend to receive donations, which enable them to keep their fees close to those of lower quality institutions. They then try to select "brighter" students, perhaps under the assumption that these people value quality more—or, at least, will add more to institutional quality. Similarly, high quality nonprofit day care centres, which frequently use donated labor and capital, often charge lower prices and have longer waiting lists than for-profit centers (Rose-Ackerman, 1983).

Hansmann and others in the asymmetric information tradition, then, have a rather sanguine view of the impact of NPO's on quality. In contrast, Newhouse (1970) takes a less favorable view. In the Newhouse model of the hospital industry, administrators must choose quality as well as quantity and their utility is

U (Quantity, Quality). Higher quality means higher costs, but does not raise revenues correspondingly and hence implies a lower equilibrium quantity (where $AC = AR$). Thus, hospital administrators face a quantity–quality tradeoff. Their preference for quality may lead them to produce fewer low quality (cheap) medical services than would be optimal, i.e., they increase quality to a point where its marginal social value is less than its marginal cost.

In support of this hypothesis, Newhouse mentions that nonprofit hospitals have more expensive, underutilized equipment than proprietary hospitals, do fewer routine and more esoteric procedures, etc. Philanthropy, he believes, increases the problem because it is often earmarked for quality. Free entry might improve matters, leading more enterprises to provide profitable low-quality services, but nonprofit status in an industry makes it difficult to raise capital and hence deters entry. As in earlier models, it is the existence of donations and entry barriers that allow the quality preference to become effective in NPO's, hence the nature of the donations function and entry conditions crucially determine their behavior.

In a comparison of the quality of nonprofit and for-profit nursing homes, Weisbrod and Schlesinger (1986) use consumer complaints to regulatory authorities as an inverse measure of quality. They find that non-profits have significantly fewer complaints and, in this limited sense, offer higher quality. Their analysis, however, does not take into account differences in cost and demand functions faced by nonprofit and proprietary nursing homes. Nonprofits benefit from tax exemptions and other cost advantages which might lead them to produce higher quality (as well as quantity) even if they were acting as profit-maximizers. They are exempt from social security, unemployment insurance, local property and sales taxes (Hansmann, 1981, Vogel, 1977) and in some situations they pay lower wages than for-profits. Thus, the apparent behavioral difference may be an artifact of our tax laws and other cost differentials, rather than stemming from different objective functions and constraints inherent in the non-profit institutional form.

Gertler (1984) tests this proposition by, in effect, turning it into an index number problem. He estimates separate demand and cost functions for proprietary and nonprofit nursing homes, and calculates the quality of care that profit-maximizers would provide if they had the nonprofit cost and demand structures. He finds that, under these conditions, quality would be higher than it is in reality either for NPO's or PMO's. This implies that nonprofit objectives and constraints and for-profit cost and demand structures both depress quality. In his study, the observed higher quality for NPO's, as compared with proprietary homes, is due entirely to cost and demand differences, rather than to different objectives and constraints. In fact, the NPO's actually produce lower quality (and higher quantity of care for indigent patients) than they would if they acted like profit-maximizers. His explanation is that most nonprofit nursing homes are run by religious groups, who feel an obligation to accommodate their members, many of whom cannot afford high quality (costly) care.

In many industries government production also coexists with and is the major competitor of nonprofit suppliers. In such cases, especially when viewed from an international perspective, it is by no means clear that nonprofits are the high quality providers. While generalizations are difficult, when government goods or services are aimed at the mass audience, private nonprofit services are frequently preferred as higher quality; when government services are aimed at a more narrowly restricted elite audience, private services are regarded as lower quality. For example, in countries (such as the U.S.) where government schools are open access, the elite schools are private; where government schools are selective (as in much of the world), private nonprofit schools spring up to meet the excess demand and these are considered lower quality by most commonly used indices (exam performance of incoming and outgoing students, expenditures per student, student/faculty ratios, etc.). (The distinction between gross output and value added, quality versus efficiency, in this connection, is discussed in James 1984a and 1986b, James and Benjamin, 1984). Again, in the health industry, in many countries government hospitals directed at special privileged groups (the armed forces, social security recipients) are most preferred, govenment hospitals for the masses are least preferred, and proprietary hospitals are viewed as an extension of a private doctor's practice, often providing high quality care. In contrast, nonprofit hospitals offer neither the personalization of the proprietary clinics nor the high technology of the specialized government institutions, and therefore fall somewhere in the middle of the spectrum between these institutions and low quality public hospitals.

Thus, empirical work from a variety of industries and countries corroborates the hypothesis that NPO's behave differently from PMO's or government, but one cannot assume that NPO's necessarily supply the highest quality.

D. The multi-product NPO

1. *The basic model.* Some of the conclusions in the previous sections are reversed when we consider the case of the multi-product NPO (James 1978, 1983, 1986a, James and Neuberger, 1981). This model demonstrates the likelihood of cross-subsidization, i.e., the NPO will earn a profit on some products, which it then spends on other loss-making products. Thus, the NPO behaves exactly like the PMO for some goods, may produce lower quantity or quality than the PMO for other goods, and may also exhibit backward-bending supply curves, which respond negatively to increases in product price or donations.

In the simplest formulation of the two-product model, the NPO manager maximizes his/her utility $U(Q_1, Q_2)$ subject to the zero profit constraint $(P_1 + D_1)Q_1 + (P_2 + D_2)Q_2 + FR - C(Q_1) - C(Q_2) = 0$, where P_i, D_i are the price and (public or private) donations paid for each unit of Q_i and FR is the "fixed revenue" from lump-sum donations or subsidies. The first-order conditions, when appropriately rearranged, are:

$$\frac{\partial U/\partial Q_1}{\partial U/\partial Q_2} = \frac{\partial C/\partial Q_1 - (P_1 + D_1)}{\partial C/\partial Q_2 - (P_2 + D_2)}$$

That is, the marginal rate of substitution between Q_1 and Q_2 equals their relative net marginal costs. This may be contrasted with the equilibrium position of the PMO, where $dC/dQ_i = (P_i + D_i)$ for Q_1 and Q_2.

If we compare the equilibrium quantities of the NPO (denoted Q_i^*) and the PMO (denoted $\bar{Q}_i$) we observe the following:

(1) If $\partial U/\partial Q_i = 0$, then $Q_i^* = \bar{Q}_i$. The nonprofit and profit maximizer both choose the same quantity, the point of "maximum potential profits" for product i. Such activities may be termed "pure production."

(2) If $\partial U/\partial Q_i > 0$, $Q_i^* > \bar{Q}_i$. The nonprofit produces more than the profit maximizer because its manager derives positive utility

from Q_i. It is obviously possible, in such cases, for the nonprofit to make a financial loss on product i. These utility-yielding activities are called "implicit organizational consumption."

(3) If $\partial U/\partial Q_i < 0$, $Q_i^* < \bar{Q}_i$. The nonprofit produces less than the profit-maximizer, because these activities are a source of disutility. Moreover, the NPO produces disutility-yielding levels of Q_i only if it is profitable. These activities are "joint production-negative consumption" and may have a backward-bending supply curve.

Thus, the NPO engages in some (production) activities which it then uses to finance its utility-yielding (consumption) activities. High quality or esoteric medical care (as in Newhouse) would be an example of loss-making "organizational consumption" in nonprofit hospitals which is subsidized by the more routine profitable cases in which proprietary hospitals specialize. James argues that at American universities undergraduate education is carried out as a profit-making production activity in order to subsidize the loss-making consumption of graduate training and research that faculty-managers prefer. (PMO's would produce more of the former, less of the latter). Similarly in the arts, museum gift shops and special exhibitions are profitable activities used to cross-subsidize their loss-making permanent collections.

Of course, positive profits and cross-subsidization can be maintained in the long run only if there are barriers to entry. Otherwise, single product PMO's or NPO's specializing in profitable services which are attractive to customers and donors would be founded, eventually increasing quantity supplied enough to eliminate profits. Thus, either potential entrepreneurs willing and able to establish single-product NPO's are not available (see Part V) or else there are so many economies from joint production that clients still believe they are better off dealing with a multi-product firm.

2. *Reaction of multi-product NPO's to changes in donations and product price.*   The same utility-maximizing process that leads to cross-subsidization also causes NPO's to react in curious and often unpredictable ways to changes in financing arrangements and economic incentives. Specifically, we find backward-bending supply

curves, negative responses to lump-sum donations or subsidies, and non-zero cross-elasticities of supply, even in the absence of technological interdependencies. As a result, NPO behavior may differ from that expected by the private donor or government planner who is providing the financing. This throws further light on whether multi-product NPO's are "trustworthy."

To investigate these questions, James (1983) derives the income and substitution effects for the multi-product NPO. She finds that lump sum donations not tied to the production of particular outputs will increase the output of goods preferred by managers, decrease those they dislike, and have no impact on pure production, where NPO's behave just like PMO's. Even if the grants are tied to particular NPO programs, donors must check to be sure the tied money does not simply replace untied funds, permitting the NPO to treat the gift like a lump-sum grant.

Recall that, in our earlier discussion, we presented theories of NPO formation which stressed donor willingness to contribute to NPO's. In the absence of monitoring, NPO's were considered more trustworthy, more likely to spend the donations to increase output, rather than to generate a surplus. We now confirm that this holds for some NPO goods, but not for all; in fact, the provision of production-negative consumption will actually fall, when lump sum donations increase. The resulting allocation and output effect, therefore, may be very different from the donor's intent; his trust may have been misplaced.

One can extend this analysis by viewing the government very much like a giant multi-purpose nonprofit organization. In such an organization, the ability of potential donors to predict the use of their donations is very small. Thus over and above the familiar free rider problem, this phenomenon helps explain why government rarely attracts donations, even though it produces public goods with positive externalities: individuals might derive utility from increasing some of the government's activities, but they may derive little or negative utility from other activities and cannot predict which service will be increased by their donations. An NPO, even though multi-product, has a much more narrowly restricted range of options, so potential donors know approximately what their money will be spent on. If the donor has a strong preference for the general class of activities carried on by the NPO and only weak preference among them, he may be willing to contribute, despite his inability to control or even monitor the precise use of his money. (In contrast to their unwillingness to donate money to government, people may be willing to donate time, since they can directly monitor and control the allocation of their time donations. Thus, the phenomenon of volunteers in public schools or public hospitals is not inconsistent with the above paragraph.)

NPO's also face revenue changes stemming from changes in product price paid directly by consumers or by government on their behalf. The impact on Q_i of a change in its own price, $\partial Q_i / \partial P_i$, depends on both an income and a substitution effect. The substitution effect is always positive. However, as we saw above, the income effect may be greater or less than zero, depending on the marginal utility of the good to the NPO manager. As a consequence of these two forces, James shows that the "own price effect," $\partial Q_i / \partial P_i$, is positive if marginal utility equals zero, because of the substitution effect; is positive if marginal utility exceeds zero, due both to the income and substitution effects; is ambiguous in sign if marginal utility is negative, since the income and substitution effects move in opposite directions. In the latter case, if the income effect dominates, Q_i will have a backward-bending supply curve so higher prices will, perversely, cause it to produce less, not more. This suggests that, for some goods, NPO's will be very unresponsive to increases in demand from customers or donors.

An investigation of $\partial Q_i / \partial P_j$ yields an even more complex pattern of income and cross-substitution effects, depending both on $\partial U / \partial Q_i$ and $\partial U / \partial Q_j$. This implies that the output of a good may change in a positive or negative direction even if its own costs and demand are unchanged, making it very difficult to predict NPO behavior.

To illustrate these effects, suppose that a wealthy philanthropist gives an unrestricted grant to a private university. We assume that this grant is unrestricted by the donor or, because of the fungibility of money, it can be treated as if it were unrestricted. We would predict that research and graduate training (organizational consumption) will increase, undergraduate enrollments (joint production-negative consumption) will decrease, and real estate investments (pure production) will remain unchanged. If the philanthropist expected his money to be spent on undergraduate education, he would be disappointed by these results—but, given the monitoring problems, he probably would never know. If government support for research increases, it would have similar effects to those just described. However, if market tuition (or state subsidy) per undergraduate increases, the net outcome is difficult to predict. If the substitution effect dominates, undergraduate enrollments will rise, but if the income effect dominates, universities end up admitting higher quality, hence a lower quantity of students; there is a backward-bending supply curve of undergraduate places. In this case, the non-profit sector is totally unresponsive to increases in demand.

Empirical evidence does indicate that nonprofits respond slower than for-profits to increased demand. In industries where both nonprofits and for-profits play an important role, the market share of the former is lower in markets where demand has been expanding rapidly (Steinwald and Neuhauser, 1970, Hansmann, 1982). The reluctance of old institutions to expand and the difficulties in raising capital for new NPO's also helps explain why public production is preferred to private nonprofit production in some instances, e.g. when many new state universities were built to accommodate the baby boom entering American higher education in the 1960's (James, 1978, 1986a).

E. Summary: nonprofits versus for-profits

In sum, we have seen that, under certain conditions, nonprofit managers have a greater opportunity to engage in discretionary behavior than their PMO counterparts. This opportunity stems from two factors: 1) the existence of lump sum donations, i.e. donations which are not contingent on specific output, either because they have not been earmarked or cannot be monitored (this is particularly likely to be the case if contributions are in the form of money, not time, and if donors are small and dispersed); and 2) barriers to entry, such as accreditation requirements, reputation or legal requirements of nonprofit status. Lump sum donations and entry barriers create "potential profits" even in the long run, and these can then be "spent" by NPO managers on activities that enter directly into their utility functions. In this sense, NPO managers have property rights over their choice of inputs and outputs, which they can use to enhance their own welfare, within limits set by these "potential profits." Examples of preferred activities that we have discussed above include: shirking and x-inefficiency (less managerial effort), technological preference, high quality production or cross-subsidization of services preferred by managers. The behavior of the nonprofit firm may thus be different from that intended by the public or private donors, who created the potential profits in the first place. We found that nonprofit quantity and quality may be greater or less than that in a PMO. We also observed a potential trade-off between the social goals of increased output and productive efficiency.

Of course, the more nonprofit managers exercise their discretion in opposition to the preferences of their customers, the less competitive they become with PMO's in the same general area of demand. For example, the more NPO hospitals engage in fancy esoteric treatment, the more room they leave in the market for PMO's to carry out profitable routine treatment. In this sense, larger lump-sum donations and subsidies to NPO's also create a market niche for PMO's, because of the negative income effect upon the supply of goods which are a source of disutility to NPO managers. Thus, as government subsidies to European nonprofit cultural organizations increased, they could more readily disregard consumer preferences, thereby paving the way for the growth of the for-profit popular theater (Montias, 1981).

5. MODELS OF NPO BEHAVIOR: IDEOLOGY, RESOURCES AND COMPETITION

The models in Part IV assume that there is an efficient way to produce output and that profit maximizing firms in competitive markets will make the correct choice. In equilibrium, marginal cost equals price, no shirking occurs, product quality reflects consumer preferences, and input and output proportions are efficient. That part of the paper thus emphasizes the failures of NPO operation relative to the benchmark of the competitive market. However, as we stressed in Part III, such a standard of comparison is inappropriate in those sectors where NPO's are prevalent, since these sectors may not fulfill the conditions needed for profit maximization to product optimal outcomes. Thus, we have a choice between two different kinds of nonoptimalities, those associated with the lack of incentives in NPO's and those associated with competitive market (or government) failure. The fact that most services supplied by nonprofits are also provided by PMO's or government agencies, and that market shares vary from one country to another, suggests that no one of these institutional forms has a clear efficiency advantage, even in the "nonprofit" industries identified in Part II. In which of these situations, then, will nonprofits flourish?

In this section we emphasize one factor that is crucial in determining when nonprofits will attract the entrepreneurs, funds and consumers to win out in this competitive struggle. We believe that a key feature of nonprofit production is ideology. This may stem from religious faith, from a secular vision of a just society, from a belief in a particular theory of education or child development, to name just a few possible sources. True, some organizations are nonprofit simply because their organizers think it will help them raise voluntary contributions or because it will bring them subsidies and tax advantages. But many organizations are nonprofit because their founders have a set of strongly felt beliefs which motivate them more than money alone. The kind of services they chose to produce, the consumers who prefer these services, as well as the NPO fundraising efforts are directly tied to the founders' beliefs. However, donors, customers and subsidies are not available to support all ideological positions equally well. Founders then face a difficult tradeoff: A tension between financial viability and principle is one of the distinguishing characteristics of many NPO's.

A. Entrepreneurship

In economic theory, ownership claims to the residual and the right to sell these claims, are the primary incentives for entrepreneurship and venture capital in modern market economies. Who provides the entrepreneurship and venture capital when these property rights do not exist, and what do they hope to gain? Will there always be a sufficient supply of nonprofit-motivated entrepreneurs ready to respond to demand? The dominance of PMO's over NPO's in most parts of our economy, particularly where capital requirements are large, suggests that their formation is indeed constrained by a lack of capital and entrepreneurs. Nonprofits are concentrated in labor-intensive service industries with relatively low capital requirements, e.g. health, education and social services. While nonprofit entrepreneurs are sometimes the recipients of "disguised profit distributions," e.g. in the form of wages and expense accounts above going market rates, the opportunities for such payments are limited. Thus, NPO entrepreneurs seem to have different motivations from their PMO counterparts and constraints on their supply may exert a powerful influence on the areas (both geographic and industrial) in which non-profits will emerge.

Young (1981, 1983, 1984) has carried out a series of detailed case studies of nonprofit entrepreneurs in the American social service industry, which show a wide range of motivations and backgrounds. He characterizes entrepreneurs as artists, professionals, believers, searchers, independents, conservers, power seekers, controllers and income seekers, and argues that people with different entrepreneurial traits will be attracted to different types of firms or industries. His underlying idea is that people care about many things besides money and may start nonprofit organizations to pursue their nonpecuniary goals. In a follow-up study Legorreta and Young (1986) examined several organizations that had changed from the for-profit to the nonprofit form of organization. They argue that these shifts permitted an entrepreneur with a commitment to a particular vision of the organization's mission to preserve that vision while relinquishing day-to-day control. This observation may have more general applicability. The nonprofit corporate form may be a way for an organization to grow and obtain limited liability without leaving itself open to takeover by profit-oriented raiders. This is not to say that fights for control do not occur in the nonprofit sector but only to claim that one set of contestants, those concerned with maximizing profits, will be excluded.

James, in her study of nonprofit organizations around the world, found that most founders of NPO's are not randomly drawn individuals seeking personal gain but, rather, are "ideological" organizations—political groups, Socialist labor unions and, first and foremost, organized religion (James, 1982a, 1984a, 1986b). In country after country, religious groups are the major founders of nonprofit service institutions. Religious groups provide the organizational ability, the venture capital and, often, low paid or volunteer labor as well. This supply-side variable suggests that NPO's will be more important in countries with strong, independent proselytizing religious organizations competing for clients, and there is some empirical evidence to support this hypothesis. In a regression analysis explaining regional differences in the size of the private sector in education, an indicator of religious entrepreneurship turned out to be significant in a variety of modern and developing countries (James, 1984b).

This observation also explains why nonprofits are concentrated in industries such as education and health and suggests a particular reason why the nonprofit form was chosen by the founders. Their object was not to maximize profits but to maximize religious faith or religious adherents, and schools are one of society's most important institutions of taste formation and socialization. Similarly, hospitals are a service for which people have an urgent periodic need and hence constitute an effective way for religious groups to gain entree and good will in a society.

James argues that the nonprofit form was chosen by the founders because their main objective was · often not compatible with profit-maximizing behavior or even with the appearance of profit-maximizing behavior. For example, religious schools set up to keep members within the fold and/or attract new believers, may have to charge a price below the profit-maximizing level in order to entice the largest numbers in. For proselytizing reasons, they may wish to present an image of service and dedication, rather than appear "self-serving" and profit-seeking. The nondistribution constraint conveys this image, at little cost to an organization which did not intend to make large profits anyway. It also reduces the monitoring problems faced by the upper church hierarchy in cases where lower-level church officials are managing these service institutions.

Once these religious nonprofits are founded, they have a comparative advantage over their secular competitors, both nonprofit and for-profit. First, they have a semi-captive audience in members of the religious organization; such customers may "trust" them precisely because they are run by religious groups, not because of their nonprofit legal status. Second, they have access to low cost volunteer labor (e.g. priests and nuns) and monetary contributions of churchgoers, which allow them to undercut their private secular rivals and compete with government services. (In fact, religious organizations were the traditional basis for collective action and public goods long before secular nation states existed.) Third, the religious group may be politically powerful enough to secure government subsidies and to require (as an anti-competitive device) that only nonprofits be eligible for these subsidies. Thus, the availability of religious or other ideological entrepreneurs may be viewed as a supply-side variable that supplements the market and planning failure arguments of Part III, in explaining where the nonprofit form is used and how NPO's compete effectively with public or profit-maximizing alternatives.

B. Variety

When nonprofits compete with government bureaucracies, theory predicts that NPO's will offer a variety of services in the face of a relatively uniform government product. Thus, the nonprofit form develops to accommodate diverse consumer tastes. However, it is not clear that NPO's will perform better than PMO's when product variety is valuable to consumers. In fact, the discussion of entrepreneurship in the preceding section leads us to suspect that founders and managers may have strong ideological beliefs which do not precisely match the set of consumer preferences.

Rose-Ackerman (1982a, 1983a) develops a model along these lines in which nonprofits are founded and managed by ideological people with strong preferences for particular qualities (e.g. an elementary school run on Catholic principles, an art school based on a particular theory of painting, a mental hospital run by doctors with a strong commitment to Freudian analysis). Because of informational asymmetries, PMO's are not able to survive; because of the nondistribution constraint, only ideological entrepreneurs are attracted to the nonprofit sector, and because of economies of scale, every possible ideological preference need not be represented. This combination of conditions implies that entrepreneurs with the most intense ideological beliefs will be overrepresented in such industries. Founder/managers may compromise their principles somewhat in order to obtain enough funds to survive. However, limitations on entry give managers the discretion to accommodate their own strong ideological preferences. Thus, the mixture of services that actually exists may not be an accurate reflection of the preferences of donors and customers and this may be a stable result because of the small number of potential entrants and the costs of entry.

The possible mismatch of NPO product variety and customer or donor tastes is similar to the results obtained in models of local government provision of quasi-public goods. The Tiebout hypothesis proposes that people will move to a geographic community offering the kinds of services they prefer, and new communities will spring up to accommodate diverse preferences. However, economies of scale and other barriers to entry and mobility may stop this process of community formation before all tastes are satisfied (Rose-Ackerman, 1983c). NPO's may then be considered a "community of interest" which constitute an alternative to geographically-based communities, providing variety without movement. The ideological motivation for founding nonprofits, however, provides an additional reason, not important in the local government context, why NPO's are an imperfect mechanism for responding to heterogeneous consumer tastes.

C. Fundraising

Nonprofits cannot survive on the strong ideological beliefs of their founders and managers alone. They also need resources. Even an organization founded by people who deplore the materialism of society must obtain ongoing financial support. Thus, just as a PMO engages in advertising to raise revenues through product sales, an NPO engages in fundraising to raise donations. These fundraising campaigns are likely to stress the religious or ideological point of view of the organizations. Contributions may then be provided which translate into tangible benefits such as education or social interaction, or intangible benefits such as salvation, social standing, or assuagement of a guilty conscience. When the latter motivations are important, strongly ideological organizations may have a comparative advantage in obtaining donations over other groups with a poorly thought out underlying philosophy. NPO's will then allocate a portion of their budget to informing potential donors both about the actual programs they are carrying out and about their point of view.

  Given its ideological position, an organization that wishes to maximize resources net of fundraising costs will invest in fundraising until the marginal dollar spent produces just one dollar in expected gifts. On the margin, the fundraising share is 100%. The problem of choosing the optimal amount of fundraising is more complex than the question of optimal advertising because donors may care about fundraising shares and may be less likely to donate to charities if they believe their donation will be spent on fundraising rather than final output (cf. Tullock, 1966). To model fundraising activities, then, we first must model donor behavior, or, at least, NPO beliefs about donor behavior.

Let us call fundraising expenses as a percent of total revenues A; suppose (nonprofits think that) donors believe that $A\%$ of each donation will be spent on fundraising; and suppose further that each individual who learns about an NPO gives less as A increases. This exerts a dampening effect on A, the average fundraising share. However, as A increases more people learn about (and potentially donate to) the NPO—the positive effect of A. Weisbrod and Dominguez (1986) have shown empirically that donors are influenced positively by advertising and negatively by the fundraising percentage of nonprofits. These two forces interact to determine an equilibrium level of A that maximizes total revenues net of fundraising expenses.

Steinberg (1986a, 1986b) has argued that donors of small amounts of money should *not* consider A, average fundraising costs, in deciding whether to donate because these expenses are independent of their own gifts. A marginal contribution will be used 100% for programs. As Steinberg shows, this result must be modified if the donor is "large." The contributor should then take account of the impact of his gift on fundraising expenses and, ultimately, on the gifts of others. If donors believe fundraising is productive (i.e. highly revenue-yielding), they may actually give more if they anticipate that part of their gift will be used for fundraising, thereby generating additional resources for the charity.

Alternatively, some donors may believe that by making a gift they can psychologically "buy in" to the entire program of the charity. Then, ceteris paribus, charities that spend little on fundraising but have the same total revenue are preferred to those that spend a lot. In short, the NPO faces a complex decision-making task: To determine fundraising expenditures it must model donor behavior, which depends in part on donor beliefs about NPO fundraising behavior, making this an exceedingly difficult problem for numerous decentralized and dispersed NPO's to solve.

The above analysis considers each charity in isolation. While charities may compete with each other, these interactions are not explicitly modelled. In an attempt to capture some of these interactions, Rose-Ackerman (1982a) considers a stylized long-run case with free entry of charities at all points on the ideological spectrum whenever existing nonprofits have an excess of gifts over fundraising costs. The paradoxical result is a world in which no resources are ultimately spent on charitable services because new firms enter and compete away the gains of existing firms by additional fundraising expenditures. Even if donors disfavor charities with high fundraising shares, this is not sufficient to hold back the destructive competition.

The model is, of course, too extreme because it neglects the entry barriers that actually exist in the non-profit world. Nevertheless, it does point up a severe tension in the sector. Laissez-faire policies regarding fundraising, which make it easy for a multitude of diverse and innovative nonprofits to exist, will also make it harder for any one of them to succeed in providing a high level of services. Increased numbers mean increased competition for funds and hence increased fundraising shares which may in turn diminish net service levels. In this context, entry barriers may make things better, not worse.

United Funds (joint fundraising drives) constitute such an entry barrier through an agreement with employers to provide payroll deductions only to the United Fund. In return for membership in the Fund and access to payroll deductions, charities agree not to carry out competing fundraising drives. Fisher (1977) shows that the tying together of contributions by United Funds may increase overall donations and Rose-Ackerman (1982a) argues that insofar as the United Fund makes the establishment of new charities costly, and thereby limits fundraising costs, it may also help maintain the level of expenditures on direct service provision. Nevertheless, the United Fund has been criticized for restricting donors' freedom of choice, for retaining outdated allocation formulas, and for making it difficult for young (some controversial) organizations, responding to new community problems, to obtain membership and resources. United Funds are caught between their conflicting roles as, on the one hand, a coalition of established charities seeking to maximize service revenues and, on the other, an organization designed to help donors make intelligent contribution decisions over the entire set of charitable needs (Rose-Ackerman, 1980).

D. Market structures and competition

In concluding this section we consider how ideological nonprofits can coexist with PMO's and public agencies in industries such as child day care or nursing homes. What are the advantages and disadvantages of each institutional type with respect to inputs and what market niches does each fill? First, consider inputs.

1. Supply of entrepreneurs. For-profits attract entrepreneurs who are willing to take risk in return for the possibility of financial gain. Nonprofits attract those with ideological beliefs, e.g. religious faith, that they wish to see promulgated more broadly. The supply of entrepreneurs of each kind can vary widely by sector and over time. In general, the supply of those seeking financial rewards is probably larger than the supply of committed ideologues, but ideologues, and hence nonprofits, may be concentrated in those areas which maximize the opportunities for influencing the values and beliefs of others.

2. Access to capital. For-profits can raise funds through stock issues and may have superior access to bank loans. Nonprofits, however, face tax advantages in their exemption from the corporate income tax and may be able to obtain venture capital in the form of "seed money" from foundations, religious organizations, or wealthy philanthropists. While this may suffice for labor intensive industries, for-profits have a clear advantage where large amounts of capital are needed.

3. Access to labor. Non-profits may have access to volunteer labor, both secular and religious. Even paid workers may receive lower wages than their counterparts in PMO's in return for superior working conditions there; the discretionary power of NPO's may enable them to indulge in activities that provide a more pleasant environment, and hence yield a lower equilibrium wage in the marketplace. Other nonpecuniary benefits may be tied to the religious or philosophical orientation of the organization. Several studies suggest that workers sort themselves across the nonprofit and for-profit sectors in part on the basis of their taste for monetary remuneration versus "socially meaningful" employment (Preston, 1984b, 1985, Weisbrod, 1983, Weisbrod, Handler and Komesar, 1978). For-profit managers generally must pay going market rates for their inputs, but they may also have a greater incentive to

operate the firm efficiently. Put another way, "shirking" in the NPO may be offset by availability to them of low cost labor and vice-versa in the PMO, thereby enabling both to compete in labor-intensive areas.

Some scholars argue that nonprofits will be less responsive to market cues than for-profits. Voluntary organizations may maintain loss-making operations longer, if covered by donations or cross-subsidization. New firms may not enter rapidly when demand increases because of limitations on nonprofit entrepreneurship and capital formation, and old firms may refuse to expand, preferring instead to be more selective or to tolerate growing queues. They may also keep quality high even in those situations where clients have difficulty observing quality, simply because the managers themselves benefit from being part of a high quality operation. They may emphasize aspects of the service provision process that promulgate an ideological belief or otherwise benefit them personally but do not satisfy many clients. In the absence of entry barriers, however, nonprofits operating in this last way can be expected to lose revenues and fail in competition with for-profit suppliers unless they have offsetting benefits such as lower capital and labor costs or unless they are supported by large donors who share the manager's preferences.

Given these differences in input costs and behavior, how do industries operate where nonprofit, for-profit and government agencies coexist? Both theory and empirical observations suggest that these three organizational types frequently provide somewhat different products or serve different clientele. In the following paragraphs we pull together some of the examples mentioned earlier, in order to illustrate how demand and supply forces interact to determine the special niche occupied by each institutional form.

Basically, for-profits can only serve those who are able to pay, either because they are relatively wealthy or because they are eligible under publicly financed entitlement programs. Thus, for-profit hospitals may locate in affluent neighborhoods and specialize in "diseases of the rich." In some countries, these are extensions of a doctor's practice and are considered high quality. Government hospitals are the largest and most capital intensive, often treating a wider range of patients and diseases. Nonprofit hospitals, typically founded by religious organizations, play a relatively small role in most countries, but in the United States, Holland and several other countries they are important and perform some of the functions provided by government and private hospitals elsewhere. For example, they have been viewed either negatively, as a doctor's cooperative, designed to maximize physicians' incomes through disguised profit distribution, using insurance-fee financing as their major source of revenue (Pauly and Redisch, 1973); or, positively, as large multi-purpose organizations, which fund less profitable but socially useful activities (e.g. medical research) through cross-subsidization or donations.

The growth of the for-profit nursing home industry has been fueled by public subsidy available through Medicaid both to NPO's and PMO's. Nonprofit nursing homes existed earlier, usually started by religious organizations for their constituents, but they too have grown in number in response to these subsidies. They seem to provide higher quality service than most for-profits, but this may be due to their special demand and cost curves rather than the nondistribution constraint. For example, they may attract clients on the basis of religious affiliation and can draw on church members for volunteer help.

In day care, for-profit chains try to establish a "brand name" reputation so that they can coexist with single nonprofits that have been started by organizations such as churches, universities, or cooperative parent groups. The in-kind subsidies to the nonprofits may enable them to provide higher quality philosophically differentiated services than for-profits, allowing them to use non-price rationing, screen applicants and choose those most interesting to them, while for-profits provide standardized but lower quality service at competitive prices. Many single proprietorships also exist in day care, with minimal profits or venture capital; the entrepreneurs simply pay themselves a salary. The decision of these small entrepreneurs to incorporate as for-profit or nonprofit, or not to incorporate at all, is unlikely to influence their behavior, given the free entry and limited potential profits (Rose-Ackerman, 1983a).

In education, public facilities are the main competitors to nonprofits. The public schools provide education to the "masses" or the "elite," depending on whether they are open access or selective. The former pattern prevails in the United States, the latter in many other countries. Once the public sector establishes its clientele, the private sector responds to the rest. Where the public system is open access to everyone, a small elite private system usually develops; where the public system is very selective, many potential students may be excluded, in which case a large for-profit or nonprofit system is often found. In either case, a religious nonprofit system typically coexists with the public, providing both selective and open access schools, to maximize the number of constituents who will be able to find the type of education they desire (James, 1984a, Levy, 1986).

In areas such as culture and entertainment, a flourishing for-profit sector usually appeals to mass audiences while nonprofits appeal to more elite tastes and rely heavily on donations from people with particular beliefs about what sort of artistic activity should be encouraged. In some countries governments provide these elite cultural services. We have seen that affluence insulates nonprofit and governmental arts organizations from consumer preferences, hence allowing greater scope for the more responsive for-profit sector to develop.

How does this picture relate to our earlier discussion of nonprofit theory? Not surprisingly, for-profits exist in most areas where fees can be charged sufficient to cover the costs. They are less prevalent in areas where demand is very limited, where exclusion cannot be practiced, where provision to the needy (those unable to pay) is the goal or where the government, for some other reason, has decided to provide the service at minimal private cost.

The nonprofit sector, in contrast, can and does flourish in these very areas, particularly in those subsectors (schools, day care) where taste formation and socialization occur. It is noteworthy that the services which are provided by the nonprofit sector in one country tend to be provided by the government, more than for-profits, in other countries. Nonprofits survive because they are often motivated by ideology, rather than profits, and because they receive private donations or government subsidies to help cover their costs.

In many cases, especially in the U.S., nonprofits seem to have a quality edge over for-profits or government, as our theoretical models predicted. However, it cannot be said that nonprofits universally specialize in the high quality market niche; from an international perspective for-profit hospitals or government schools are often the preferred alternative, and in culture/entertainment the sectoral distinctions depend on taste differences rather than quality. Thus, these empirical observations give limited support to theories that emphasize nonprofits as key providers of quality, but are generally consistent with theories that stress philanthropy, public goods and financing, and religious or ideological entrepreneurship in the nonprofit sector.

6. COMPARISONS WITH OTHER PROFIT-CONSTRAINED FIRMS

Part II compared nonprofit organizations with the norm of classical profit-maximizing firms. However, scholars have frequently suggested that managers of many firms care about other goals besides just profit maximization. In fact, profits are often said to serve as a constraint, rather than a maximand. In this section we compare the behavior of the nonprofit organization with that of other private, profit-contrained institutional forms. Specifically, we consider the Baumol sales-maximizing firm (1959, 1967), the Williamson firm with expense preference (1964, 1975), and the regulated monopoly discussed by Alchian and Kessel (1962) and others. Although the rationale for each of these organizations differs, we find many behavioral similarities to NPO's, especially in their reactions to changes in revenue and costs. To the degree that profit constraint rather than profit maximization is the rule, NPO's may behave very much like other enterprises in the economy, except that they typically have ideological as well as material goals.

Discretionary behavior in the Baumol and Williamson firms stems from the familiar "separation of ownership from control" problem, currently relabelled the "principal-agent" problem. Is separation of ownership from control efficient, given that it may lead to various types of non-profit-maximizing activities? As Meckling and Jensen (1976) point out, the people with the greatest managerial skills may not be those with enough wealth for total ownership, and there are gains from risk-sharing which accrue from dispersed ownership, so separation of ownership and day-to-day management may be efficient on these grounds in complex organizations. (For similar reasons, separation of the labor and risk-bearing functions is efficient, and tying these together in the Yugoslav worker-managed enterprise may be a source of inefficiency. See Neuberger and James, 1973.) The inability of dispersed owners to monitor perfectly, and the cost of control systems, offset these advantages. The survival of large corporations suggests that the benefits often exceed the costs so, on balance, the structure may be more efficient than other feasible structures, although not as efficient as some "ideal" structures that are not feasible.

A. The Baumol sales-maximizing firm

In the Baumol sales-maximizing firm, business managers care about total revenues, rather than just net profit. Declining sales make customers, workers, distributors and bankers more difficult to deal with. Executive salaries may fall as well, since empirical evidence indicates that managerial compensation is correlated with enterprise size more than profits. The firm must, however, provide a rate of return to its stock-holders sufficient to keep the company's securities attractive in the capital market. Therefore, the Baumol firm wishes to maximize sales subject to a minimum profit constraint. Formally this means the firm maximizes PQ subject to the constraint that $PQ - C(Q) = \bar{\pi}$, where $\bar{\pi}$ is the minimum acceptable level of profits. Note that, in structure, this is very similar to the maximizing problem of the nonprofit firm, except that $\bar{\pi} = 0$ for the NPO, and this structural similarity implies the behavioural similarities that we shall find.

The Baumol firm produces to a point where

$$P + \lambda(P - \partial C/\partial Q) = 0,$$

This equation implies that $\partial C/\partial Q > P$, i.e. marginal profits are less than 0. In effect, the firm spends its potential profits to increase sales and the last dollar in profits sacrificed from each product must yield the same revenue. Diagramatically, Figure 4 shows that Q_1 is chosen to maximize revenue, rather than Q_0 which would be chosen by a PMO or Q_2 by a single-product NPO.

The Baumol model leads to several behavioral predictions which differ from those of the PMO and are strikingly similar to those of

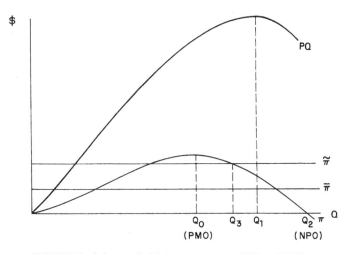

FIGURE 4   Sales-maximizing output versus NPO and PMO output.

the NPO:

1. Output is usually greater than for the PMO. If, at the point of maximum profits, marginal costs exceed zero (the usual case), this implies that marginal revenue also exceeds zero so the Baumol firm will produce additional units, so long as it remains above the minimum profit constraint. As we saw in Part IV, this is also true for consumption goods in the multi-product NPO, but it is not true for production or joint production-negative consumption goods.

2. In the long run, this difference can only remain in industries that are not perfectly competitive, hence have positive profits. Since PMO's in such industries will restrict output below the optimal level, sales maximization moves us toward efficiency. The normative evaluation of NPO's is less clear, but if market failure previously led to underproduction in these industries, increased output by NPO's also improves efficiency, decreased output makes the situation worse.

3. A rise in the minimum profit constraint reduces output in the Baumol firm. For example, if the profit constraint increases from $\bar{\pi}$ to $\tilde{\pi}$ in Figure 4, Q decreases from Q_1 to Q_3, in order to satisfy

the new constraint. The same would be true of a rise in lump sum taxes, overhead costs, or (conversely) fixed revenues, if the profit constraint is effective. In this respect, the Baumol firm is like the NPO but unlike the PMO. The reason is that, once a profit constraint is introduced, and other arguments (besides profits) enter into the objective function, an income effect influences its ability to maximize utility, so that lump-sum as well as marginal costs and revenues affect behavior. (Ironically, this also implies that the Baumol firm would react positively to donations—although philanthropists do not seem to realize this.)

4. The last dollar in profits sacrificed from each product must yield the same revenue in the Baumol firm. However if the firm produces several products, it is possible that, on average, one product may be profitable and another loss-making. In this sense, cross-subsidization is present in the sales-maximizing organization as in the NPO, although it would not be present in long-run equilibrium for the PMO.

5. On the other hand, for any given total budget, the sales-maximizing firm will allocate its expenditures among inputs in the same way a PMO would (since profits = revenue − cost, hence with costs fixed, behavior that maximizes profits also maximizes revenues). Thus, differences in the behavior of sales-maximizing and profit-maximizing firms are due to differences in total costs, not to a reallocation of given costs. In this respect, the sales-maximizing firm differs from Williamson's firm with expense preference or the NPO with technological preferences.

B. The Williamson firm with expense preference

Williamson (1964) argues that managers prefer certain expenditures over others, because these expenditures help them achieve private goals, such as security, status and professional excellence. Managers will choose to spend on these factors beyond the point justified by their contribution to profits. For example, a larger staff enhances the dominant position of a manager and may give him access to promotion. Fringe benefits and perquisites are preferred because they are less visible (and less taxable), hence can often be secured beyond the competitive wage level.

Unlike Baumol's firm, Williamson's manager likes to earn "discretionary profits" beyond the minimum constraint because this facilitates the expansion of the firm and may lead to higher salary and prestige for him. This means that the minimum profit constraint is less likely to be effective in the Williamson model, and he often ignores it. In sum, the Williamson firm wishes to maximize $U = U$ $(S, E, \pi - \bar{\pi} - T)$ subject to $\pi > (\bar{\pi} + T)$ where $S =$ expenditures on staff, $E =$ expenditures on "emoluments" (i.e. managerial salaries and perquisites beyond the minimum needed to keep the manager in his present job); $\pi =$ actual profits = revenue minus all production costs; $\bar{\pi} =$ minimum acceptable profits and $T =$ taxes.

When we compare the behavior of the expense-preference firm with that of the PMO, the sales-maximizing firm and the NPO we observe the following:

1. Like the NPO with technological preference, but unlike the Baumol firm or PMO, the Williamson firm has preferences among various inputs and hence does not act symmetrically for all of them.

2. For nonpreferred cost items (e.g. capital, which does not enter into the utility function), output is carried to the point where marginal revenue equals marginal cost. In contrast, the sales-maximizing firm or the quantity-maximizing NPO would hire factors and produce output beyond this point.

3. Preferred cost items, such as staff, are hired to a point where the marginal value product is less than marginal cost. We observe the same behavior in an NPO with technological preference.

4. Thus, output in a Williamson firm will be greater than that for a PMO, as is also the case in many NPO models.

5. The firm will also absorb some of its actual profits as emoluments (e.g. managerial fringe benefits and perks). The NPO, too, may increase managerial salary and perquisites beyond their opportunity cost, as suggested particularly in the Alchian–Demsetz model.

In sum, the NPO and Williamson firm with expense preference have many characteristics in common, including the tendency to favor certain factors of production and to increase (certain) outputs beyond the profit-maximizing levels. In both cases, these differences from PMO behavior are likely to persist in the long run only if there are barriers to entry (or donations).

The expense preference firm, like the NPO and the sales-maximizing firm, will also change its behavior in response to changes in overhead costs, fixed revenues and lump sum taxes, due to an income effect. We find less output and fewer staff and emoluments if taxes or fixed costs increase, more if there are fixed revenue sources, such as donations. Again, philanthropists do not seem to react accordingly.

Williamson devotes a good deal of space to a discussion of income and substitution effects, using a change in the income tax rate as an illustrative case. As we saw in our discussion of the NPO in Part IV, the income and substitution effects often move in opposite directions, making final outcomes difficult to predict. For example, if the profits tax rate increases, the income effect would lead the Williamson firm to hire fewer staff but the substitution effect would lead it to substitute staff for profits, hence to hire more. Therefore, the net impact is uncertain. Output would move in the same direction as staff. Similarly, a rise in market wages might lead to fewer emoluments (negative income effect) or more (emoluments substituted for staff). While these precise effects do not emerge in most NPO models, the complex pattern of income and substitution effects is clearly found.

C. The regulated monopoly of Alchian and Kessel

The "regulated monopoly" of Alchian and Kessel turns out to be very similar to the Williamson firm behaviorally, although its origin may be quite different. In the Alchian and Kessel model, discretionary profits are the preferred goal of managers, but they also have other arguments in their utility function, as in the Williamson model. A maximum profit constraint is imposed by external political forces (rather than a minimum constraint stemming from market forces, as in Williamson). Once this constraint is reached, higher potential profits are ruled out and are, in effect, traded off for other activities (such as perquisites, emoluments, shirking, nepotism) that yield direct managerial utility. Thus, the regulated monopoly behaves like the NPO, whose maximum allowable (distributed) profits are zero, and the firm with expense preference, only more so. In particular, once the constraint is effective, the system is even further removed from the profit-maximizing position than the Williamson firm, since the opportunity cost of staff and emoluments in terms of potential profits foregone is now zero. Also, when the constraint is effective, changes in lump sum taxes, costs and revenues, will affect behavior via the income effect, and price changes among the arguments in the utility function will have both substitution and cross-substitution effects, as in the expense preference firm and the NPO.

D. General observations

Testable hypotheses (e.g. about signs of income and substitution effects) emerge from each of these hypotheses, but these tests are difficult to implement. Baumol, Williamson, Alchian and Kessel present impressionistic evidence, and Williamson presents some corroboratory statistical results as well. However, it is difficult to prove empirically how valid these are as models of behavior in the real world.

From a theoretical point of view, it has been argued that these discretionary effects will not be found in unregulated markets, when there is no limit on the right to distribute profits and transfer ownership, because of natural selection: only profit-maximizers will survive in long run competitive equilibrium. Even if competition is limited in the product markets, competition in capital markets will accomplish the same thing; takeovers will occur if managers do not pursue profit-maximization policies.

But Williamson (1964) maintains that capital markets are also imperfect so room for discretionary behavior remains. Some of this behavior may be unobservable by others and hence attainable at zero opportunity cost to managers. So long as profits exceed some minimum acceptable amount, stockholders do not revolt nor do outsiders realize that this is fertile field to takeover—especially since they, too, will be unable to minutely monitor their managers. Also, managers may be able to discourage takeovers by raising their costs through devices such as the "golden parachute," which guarantee executives large monetary pay-offs in such cases. Finally, takeovers involve high costs for uncertain returns, while stock sales are certain and inexpensive.

At any rate, our purpose in this monograph is not to evaluate the theoretical and empirical evidence on whether sales-maximizing, expense preference and regulated firms play an important role in the economy, but simply to demonstrate the ways in which these firms are similar to and different from the NPO. Behaviorally, we found that opportunities for discretionary behavior in both types of firms permit managers to choose different input and output quantities from those in profit-maximizing firms. One important difference stems from the labor market: managers in the for-profit sector may be selected for different characteristics and values from those in the nonprofit sector, hence their objective functions and choices (with regard to variables such as quality, preferred product mix, etc.) may be correspondingly different. To analyze this would require an empirical comparison of hiring and compensation procedures and criteria in the two sectors.

Another important difference is that the NPO has announced its zero-distribution constraint publicly, often substituting ideological for pecuniary motivation, while the Baumol and Williamson firms have not done so. The NPO must, therefore, expect to gain from this announcement, while the Baumol and Williamson firms do not expect to gain and may, in fact, lose. These firms, of course, are not "supposed to" be limiting profits in favor of other maximizing objectives, ideological or otherwise. In fact, this places them in a conflict of interest with their stockholders, who would not support the managers' goals. NPO's may gain trust and private donations, while the sales maximizing and expense preference firms would lose (stockholder) trust if they made this announcement. (And the regulated firm is regulated precisely because it might otherwise maximize its profits beyond the externally imposed limit.) Thus, although in actuality all these organizations might react in similar ways (increasing staff, output, etc.) to increases in fixed revenue, only the NPO is in a position to state this, and reap any resulting philanthropic benefits.

7. PUBLIC BUREAUCRACY AND PRIVATE NONPROFITS

The private nonprofit sector is small and insignificant compared with the other group of nonprofit organizations: government agencies or bureaus. These organizations also have no "owners" and face a nondistribution constraint that is even more severe than that facing private nonprofits. Government bureaus are generally required to turn over any surplus to the public treasury at the end of the fiscal year; they cannot save it to spend the next year as nonprofits can. The difference between public agencies and private nonprofits is not always sharp or easy to see, given the large amounts of public money filtered through nonprofits and the recent proliferation of quasi-governmental entities established by statute as private nonprofits but with substantial public financing and influence. In spite of those difficulties of definition, we will contrast purely public agencies with private nonprofits along several dimensions and consider the applicability of models of public bureaucracy to the study of private nonprofits. Most of the discussion of public bureaucracy deals with the American context, although some of it is generic. We consider models of the top officials' objective functions; their dealings with Congress, the President and the Courts; internal organizational issues; and the role of competition.

A. Objective functions

William Niskanen spawned a set of maximizing models of bureaucratic behavior. In his *Bureaucracy and Representative Government,* he claimed that top officials wish to maximize total budgets. In variants proposed by his critics and later accepted, in part, by Niskanen, the agency head maximizes discretionary budget or a more general objective funct)n where budget size is only one argument (Breton and Wintrobe, 1975, Migue and Belanger, 1974, Niskanen, 1975). Others have taken agency survival or budget maintenance to be the crucial aim (Arnold, 1979). Thus in an uncertain world an agency head would try to maximize the agency's chance of surviving or avoiding budget cuts rather than maximizing the expected budget.

Another line of research views officials as more passive. They want to avoid trouble in the form of court challenges or legislative oversight hearings. They may, however, be "captured" by the organized interest groups most concerned with agency policy and by the members of Congress most important to the future prosperity of the agency. Finally, of course, bureaucrats can be viewed either as mechanically carrying out Congress's statutory mandates or as policy entrepreneurs with strong ideological commitments to particular policies or points of view. (For a review of this literature see Posner, 1981).

All of these various objective functions have parallels in work on non-profits. As we pointed out in Parts IV and V, non-profit managers have considerable discretion to ignore customer and donor preferences and to maximize their own objective function, which may include arguments such as quantity, quality, perquisites and product type. In several of Rose-Ackerman's papers (1981, 1982a) she assumes that nonprofit managers maximize revenue or revenue minus fundraising costs given an ideological position. The opposite extreme of maximizing an ideological goal subject to a survival constraint is one of several possibilities considered by Young (1983, 1984) in his case studies of social service agencies. Other work analyzes cases in which the nonprofit, like the public agency, is "captured" by one group with a strong interest in the organization's behavior. For example, the tenured faculty at a university may make allocation decisions that maximize the time spent on research and graduate training, two activities they prefer (James, 1978, James and Neuberger, 1981) and the hospital may operate as a physicians' cooperative designed to maximize doctors' income (Pauly and Redisch, 1973).

B. Relations with funding sources

The distinctive features of public bureaucracies relative to private nonprofits become clear when we examine the agencies' relationships to their funding sources. In contrast to most operating nonprofits, federal agencies generally have a single source of funds: congressional appropriations. Even though in the U.S. agency heads must negotiate with the Office of Management and Budget (OMB) in the Executive Office of the President and with several Congressional committees, the process of obtaining funds ultimately reduces to a single budgetary choice. A few federal agencies do rely on fees or earmarked taxes and at the state and local levels intergovernmental grants complicate the process of obtaining resources. Nevertheless, even for such agencies the problem is not nearly so complex and open-ended as a nonprofit's search for support from donors, public grants, fees and associated profit making activities.

Given the importance of the government budgetary process to public bureaus, one important issue is the ease with which the legislature or the White House can monitor agency behavior. Niskanen (1971) makes an extreme assumption: the funding source (i.e. Congress) can observe output with certainty but knows nothing about internal organization. This is quite different from the assumption usually made about NPO's and, as Breton and Wintrobe (1975) have pointed out, it is very unrealistic. In practice, members of Congress can decide how much monitoring to do based on the costs and benefits of control, with their behavior determined by the measurability of certain things and the illusiveness of others (Lindsay, 1976). In fact, Niskanen's assumption may be more appropriate for some nonprofits, such as performing arts organizations, where individual donors have little incentive to monitor internal arrangements but where everyone can observe the ultimate outcome.

Fiorina and Noll (1978) stress the collusive relationship that may develop between Congress and the bureaucracy. They argue that members of Congress are reelected, in part, because of "casework" for their constituents. Much of this casework involves intervening with government agencies on behalf of constituents. Thus, ex-ante, Congress passes laws that will require casework ex-post and agencies support these efforts because such laws will give agency officials leverage with Congress. This behavior undermines the ostensibly democratic, majoritarian nature of Congressional control. In contrast, most nonprofits do not pretend to follow democratic principles and large donors to nonprofit institutions can have considerable direct impact on programs. For example, donors might seek to undermine meritocratic selection procedures in selective colleges and graduate schools by influencing individual admissions decisions. One wonders if a study of this phenomenon would produce the same results as Mashaw's (1983) study of Congressional influence on Federal Social Security disability claims. Mashaw found that Congressional influence did not change the final result but merely made the process more cumbersome and time consuming.

A third related line of research considers the freedom of action of regulatory agencies nominally under Congressional control. Some detailed analyses of agency behavior stress the importance of personalities and organizational factors within the agency (Kaufman, 1981, Katzman, 1980). Other recent empirical work, however, claims to demonstrate that regulatory agencies such as the Federal Trade Commission and the Securities and Exchange Commission shift their behavior as the composition of Congress and especially of the oversight committees change (Moran and Weingast, 1983). This work is, to our mind, less conclusive than its authors claim, but it does make the plausible argument that the political climate in Congress affects agency behavior even for regulatory agencies which do not spend large amounts of money. Nonprofits may face similar but more attenuated pressures as broad ideological shifts in the population are reflected in donation decisions.

The role of the Executive Office of the President and the courts has also been the focus of recent work, especially as the President has moved to require more cost-benefit analysis of cabinet level regulatory agencies (e.g. Viscusi, 1983). Control of spending agencies through the Office of Management and Budget (OMB) is a longstanding practice that has been the subject of considerable analysis. However, the role of the courts in overseeing administrative agency behavior, while a central concern of work in administrative law, has been neglected by social scientists. One recent exception is a book by Melnick (1983) on the response of the Environmental Protection Agency to a series of court decisions. The book emphasizes the unintended consequences of court decisions that flowed from the court's poor understanding of technological and bureaucratic realities. Neither of these strands of research have a counterpart in the study of nonprofits, which operate under much less legal scrutiny.

Thus, in contrast to the large body of literature on the control and monitoring of public agencies by Congress, the President and the Courts, the corresponding literature on the nonprofit sector is quite thin. The basic difference is that few nonprofit agencies operate under specific enabling statutes or depend for all their resources on legislative appropriations. The main sources of oversight for non-profits are donors, through boards of directors, or the direct observation of volunteers and federated fundraising organizations. The regulatory role of government agencies, particularly when the NPO receives public subsidies, is discussed in Part VIII.

Earlier parts of this essay have dealt at length with possible conflicts between NPO managers and the donors and customers who provide the funds. Like cabinet officials and members of regulatory commissions, managers, who may also be an organization's founders, are likely to feel that they should be able to pursue their own goals to a substantial extent. So long as the organization is not controlled by a few major donors, managers are unlikely to accept directives from them and therefore have greater latitude than their public counterparts. Nonprofits, like for-profits, benefit from the existence of multiple funding sources each representing only a small portion of the total. (However, unless a nonprofit organizations has an endowment, year to year survival may be more uncertain than for a public agency.)

Some observers have claimed that federated fundraising organizations such as the United Fund can monitor the behavior of nonprofits much like OMB or a legislative oversight committee. The problem, however, is that United Fund organizations have dual, conflicting roles. On the one hand, they facilitate donations by consolidating fundraising campaigns and providing a "guarantee" of fiscal responsibility to donors. On the other hand, they are a cartel of charities reluctant to add members unless the newcomers will generate increases in total giving large enough so that existing members benefit. Under this view, the United Fund is designed to facilitate fundraising by agencies, not monitor their behavior. These conflicting goals are quite obvious when one examines the largely unsuccessful attempts by individual United Funds to monitor member agencies. In general, such monitoring is very limited and along any dimension one considers important (program choice, selection of personnel, organizational structure), United Fund member agencies are likely to have relatively more freedom of action than their public sector colleagues with the same level of resources (Rose-Ackerman, 1980).

C. Internal organization

Public bureaucracies are usually modeled as formally hierarchical organizations responsible to a democratic political body. While recent work (Breton and Wintrobe, 1982) recognizes the importance of informal alliances outside the nominal chain of command, the background structure remains hierarchical. Considerable work has been done on the use of incentives to induce lower level agents in a hierarchy to act in the interests of their principles or superiors by introducing rewards for correct decisions or penalties for incorrect ones. When superiors cannot directly evaluate low-level decisions, review processes involving an intermediate layer of the bureaucracy can be used to control low-level officials. Bureaucrats can be rewarded for decisions proven correct on appeal and penalized for those overturned at the second level (Rose-Ackerman, 1986). To the extent that nonprofit organizations are also hierarchically organized, such procedures could be implemented there as well. For example, an academic department that recommended for tenure people eventually turned down by university wide committees might find its allocation of faculty slots reduced.

However, in contrast to hierarchical public agencies, large nonprofit organizations are frequently more complex and difficult to characterize. Consider, for example, such large nonprofits as universities, hospitals, opera companies and social welfare agencies. The lack of clear lines of hierarchy is especially striking in many of these organizations, a feature that casts doubt on attempts to find *the* objective function of the NPO and makes it equally difficult to specify a workable incentive system. For example, although in universities the trustees are nominally in charge, faculty members, especially those with tenure, have considerable freedom of action. Individual departments and schools, while they may be dependent on central university funds and allocations of faculty positions, make many independent decisions. For hospitals, the central role of doctors, who are not hospital employees, puts the hospital administrator in a precarious position relative to his or her own staff (Pauly and Redisch, 1973). A similar important role for outside artists and performers exists in cultural organizations like opera companies—a relationship which may be complicated by the short-term nature of many of these ties.

With the increased professionalization of their staff, external professional associations also play an important role in setting goals and constraints of NPO's and further undermine the internal hierarchy. For example, faculty members in different university departments, such as English and Microbiology, may follow different behavioral norms because they are concerned about their reputation and job mobility within these quite different academic disciplines. Similarly, the rules on deaccessioning of objects by museums have been drafted by the Association of Museum Directors and any director disregarding these would do so at his or her peril next time he or she tried to find another job.

Finally, in social welfare agencies and, in fact, in a wide range of nonprofits, volunteer labor is of central importance (see Table I). These people, some of whom may be major donors or otherwise closely associated with board members, may be difficult for paid employees to control. Volunteers may be essential to an organization's program, but difficult to manage because they are not financially dependent on their work in the organization. Thus work on hierarchy has limited applicability to the complex, polycentric world of many nonprofits and models of fragmented overlapping decision-making systems may be more appropriate.

D. Competition in public agencies

The final body of work on public bureaucracy of interest to students of the private nonprofit sector concerns the use of competition to stimulate efficiency. Public agencies often act as monopolists, allocating scarce benefits, and their officials have the opportunity to reap personal gain (shirking, nepotism, bribes) from this allocative power. Rose-Ackerman (1978, 1986) has written about the use of competitive pressures in public agencies to minimize incentives for corruption and to improve performance. For example, in the context of a bureau charged with allocating a scarce good, if rejected applicants are given a chance to reapply, this lowers the incentive for corrupt payments and reduces the level of those that do occur. Similarly, for police or other officials who have the power to impose cost on citizens, giving them overlapping jurisdictions can also reduce the incidence and level of bribes.

The nonprofit sector, by its very structure, lacks the strong incentives for corruption present in the public sector. In general, there is considerable competition among firms and an applicant or client turned down by one provider can apply elsewhere. Nevertheless, so long as there is nonprice rationing (as when status differences exist among universities that are not fully reflected in tuition differences) the possibility for corruption remains. Here, however, outright bribery seems uncommon. After all, gifts to an institution of higher education are tax deductible while bribes are not.

A common way to introduce competitive pressures is through a voucher system where clients receive tickets that can be exchanged for the service. In general, such services are provided by private for-profit or nonprofit suppliers but there is no necessary reason why public suppliers should not also be included. In fact, just such a mixed system is contemplated in proposals for educational vouchers. More interesting, though less commonly proposed, are proxy shopping plans where needy clients are subsidized, but only if the providers they patronize also serve mobile paying customers. The level of the subsidy would then equal the market price for the unsubsidized. The paying customers, who are presumed to be informed and mobile, bring to bear the discipline of the market in ensuring minimum levels of quality and efficiency (Rose-Ackerman, 1983b). Notice, however, that plans such as vouchers or proxy shopping, while they can be used to improve the performance of public or nonprofit organizations, in fact, undermine any justification for favoring these suppliers over their for-profit counterparts. These programs enable all suppliers to be treated symmetrically, substituting public subsidies for private philanthropy as a financing mechanism, and market competition for organizational form as a quality control mechanism.

8. POLICY ISSUES

Most federal, state and local governments throughout the world favor nonprofit firms in one way or another. In the U.S., nonprofit corporations are creatures of state law so their very existence is conditioned by the restrictiveness of state incorporation statutes. Once established as legally recognized entities, NPO's are exempted from certain regulations and taxes and are even immune from certain types of tort suits. Contributions to those organizations judged to be charitable by the Internal Revenue Service are tax deductible, an implicit tax subsidy. Furthermore, some direct government subsidy programs favor nonprofit organizations by making PMO's ineligible for aid or otherwise limiting their participation. In fact, in some cases the government may even establish formally independent NPO's to receive grant and subsidy money.

We must then evaluate the range of public subsidies to determine whether they are justified on economic efficiency grounds or whether the subsidies have shaped the level and distribution of nonprofit production in inefficient ways. Would nonprofits exist without these subsidies? Are government preferences to NPO's the result of strong majoritarian arguments in their favor or are they the result of the political clout of organized nonprofit providers and their supporters? Do the benefits given to nonprofits, whatever their justification, harm profit-seeking firms which compete with them or do NPO's, instead, substitute for public bureaucratic activity and provide desirable services that would not otherwise be produced?

A. Government grants

Grants and subsidies are the most direct means by which government supports NPO's. While public money is obviously important to the sector in the U.S., it is even more central in other countries where government financing is often the main source of nonprofit revenues. Why does the government offer such support to nonprofits? What strings are and should be attached? Is this an efficient way to provide public services? This topic has been explored at greater length by James (1982a, 1984a, 1985, 1986b). While the present analysis focuses on direct government subsidies, many of these same arguments apply to indirect tax subsidies, which are discussed in the following section.

The public finance literature sets forth the classic justifications for government spending, but has little to say about the conditions under which government versus private production is optimal. Suppose, then, that we consider an activity which is generally accepted, on economic efficiency grounds, to merit some public funding. When should it be publicly produced and when should production be delegated to the private sector? The question of delegation to NPO's should be analyzed within this broader context.

We suggested in Part III that government sometimes delegates production to the private sector in order to avoid high costs and constraints in the public sector, and sometimes chooses non-profits over for-profits to encourage donations and avoid monitoring problems. In this section we examine these arguments more closely, adding empirical evidence, and attempt a normative evaluation. For reasons we shall summarize below, production by private organizations may cost the taxpayer less. However, since political and bureaucratic control is attenuated, majoritarian wishes are more difficult to fulfill. This is especially likely to be true when an organization receives funds from a number of different public agencies, no one of which provides enough of the NPO's budget to be able to dictate behavior (Kramer, 1981). Consequently, for goods that are publicly financed we face a trade-off between productive efficiency and control, and the optimal choice depends on the nature of the goods as well as the preferences of the citizens.

Suppose that quantity and quality are easily monitored, the long term distribution of desired service can be specified, and economies of scale are small. Then, the benefits of efficiency can be reaped by delegation to either PMO's or NPO's, and this is often done, as when government purchases pencils and paper or contracts with private garbage collectors to pick up refuse. At the opposite extreme, suppose that outputs (including quality) are unobservable, economies of scale are great, and it is difficult to specify the desired distribution of service in advance. Then, direct government production is probably preferable, as is the case with the armed forces. (Also see Baumol, 1984 on this issue.) In between are more ambiguous cases, where different voters and governments will choose different combinations of efficiency and control, public versus private production, and NPO's are often preferred.

1. *Private fees and donations.*   Production may be delegated to the private sector (NPO or PMO) because government hopes to supplement public support with private financing but finds it politically difficult to impose fees. Private production is then a means of evading this political constraint on public agencies. Salamon (1984) demonstrates that as public funds for nonprofits have shrunk in the last few years, the balance has been made up partly by the increased use of fees. James (1986b) documents numerous cases from a variety of countries in which private schools, hospitals and social services are expected to cover some of their own costs through fees, while similar government produced goods

are free. This occurs particularly where excess demand has fueled the growth of the private sector. Partial public subsidies are a mechanism for responding to excess demand by encouraging private service expansion at lower taxpayer cost (Weisbrod, 1977). Is this arrangement optimal?

The answer clearly depends on the mix of public and private funding that will produce the amount and distribution of the good desired by society. On the one hand, if externalities and redistributive goals are paramount, delegating production and allocation decisions to private organizations that charge fees may be both inefficient and inequitable. On the other hand, if fee financing is justified on efficiency and equity grounds, it should be imposed regardless of whether production is by government, NPO or PMO, as a first-best solution. However, if government is unable to charge fees because of narrow political pressures, even though majoritarian or efficiency principles dictate otherwise, private production may be a second best solution.

When donations are desired as a voluntary alternative to taxes, in order to reduce tax-induced disincentive effects, then production must be delegated to NPO's rather than PMO's. However, philanthropy is small in most parts of the world, may be decreasing even in the U.S. (Roberts, 1984) and, while sometimes a valuable supplement, can hardly be regarded as a large-scale substitute for tax financing.

If the government wishes to encourage private donations, it can do this by providing matching grants. This lowers the "price" of giving and should stimulate donations. Lump sum grants, in contrast, may reduce donations if donors believe that the most important services are now paid for by the government (Abrams and Schmitz, 1978, Schiff, 1984). Roberts (1984) argues that if government spending and private donations are perfect substitutes, then donations will fall by one dollar for every dollar increase in transfers to the poor. However, Rose-Ackerman (1981) demonstrates that gifts may not fall in a more complex world where the government agency induces the nonprofit to take actions that are favored by donors, e.g. keeping better records or shifting its ideological position or mix of services in a direction which donors prefer. Furthermore, public money may encourage donations by reducing fundraising costs and permitting the NPO to realize economies of scale so that marginal donations produce larger service increments.

2. *Cost savings in the nonprofit sector.* A second major reason for government grants to nonprofits is a desire for cost-saving and efficiency. As discussed in our section on public bureaucracies, government officials, as agents, will not always act in the best interests of citizens, their principals. Government is not subject to the discipline of the market place, and may engage in shirking, nepotism, corruption, x-inefficiency and various other kinds of wasteful spending. In numerous countries studied by James (1986b), private schools and hospitals were found to have lower costs particularly lower labor costs, than their government counterparts. The same was true in a study of U.S. nursing homes by Borjas, Frech and Ginsburg (1983): religious homes had lowest costs (paid lowest wages), government highest and PMO's were in between.

The lower cost stems, in part, from lower input–output ratios in the private sector, which may either indicate lower quality or greater market-induced efficiency. But much of it is due to lower average wages. Empirical evidence demonstrates that public sector workers are often paid more than those in the private sector (see, e.g., Smith, 1977, for an analysis of U.S. data). In contrast, volunteer labor has long been characteristic of NPO's and even when volunteer labor is not used, workers may accept lower wages there. Some of the wage differential may represent a more efficient organization of the work place and some of it may simply imply that the less desirable tasks are being left to public workers, who therefore must be paid more (also see our discussion in Part V on access to low-cost labor by NPO's versus PMO's).

But a good part of the lower cost occurs because private organizations are better able to circumvent constraints imposed by civil service regulations, custom or law (James and Benjamin, 1984). These prevent government from paying market-clearing wages and allow public bureaucracies to ration scarce jobs by a variety of non-price criteria such as credentials, sex or nepotism. If these criteria are justified on quality grounds (i.e. if the higher wages enable government to attract better workers), evasion through privatized production may make things worse for society. If not justified, the first best solution (as in the case of fees) would be to remove the constraint and allow government to operate more freely in the labor market. However, this may not be politically feasible, and in that case delegation of production to the private sector may be a second best solution.

It is also possible that, given the opportunities for corruption in a monopolistic public bureaucracy, some constraints are efficient there; hiring by formal educational credentials or examination score may be one such example. But good subjective judgment, in a competitive environment, may result in the hiring of superior workers at lower cost. In that case, delegation to the private sector may be desirable on first-best grounds, wherever issues of control do not dictate otherwise.

Where the motivation is cost-saving, should production be delegated to PMO's or NPO's? Suppose that monitoring of output characteristics is imperfect and allocation is difficult to specify. Then, for the reasons given in Part III, governments may feel safer dealing with NPO's rather than PMO's. We have discussed at length in this essay the question of whether or not this trust is misplaced. A preferred alternative, for example, might be to develop methods of direct monitoring, which would then permit both NPO and PMO participation. If the object is to expand available services at least cost, theory would predict both greater efficiency for competitive PMO's and a faster response to increased demand. The rapid growth of the nursing home industry with the advent of Medicare and Medicaid bears out this claim.

3. *Delegation of control.*   So far we have been considering cases where the government delegates to save costs and reluctantly relinquishes some control to NPO's or PMO's in the process. However, in some contexts independence and decentralized control by specific nonprofit organizations is exactly what is wanted. As discussed in Part V, certain nonprofit groups (often religious) want to control schools and other social services in order to gain adherents and spread their ideology, and may engage in lobbying to obtain this control, together with full or partial government subsidies. By delegating production, the party in power gains the political support of the religious group. In many European countries the religious group itself has a strong political party, able to

implement the subsidies directly. These pressures may be particularly relevant where culturally differentiated tastes for quasi-public goods have motivated the growth of the private sector.

In the United States, to help preserve the value of freedom of speech, publicly supported television and radio stations are established as nonprofit corporations. In other areas such as child day care or college training, the diversity of educational and child rearing philosophies made possible in part by the subsidy of NPO's gives people a choice and contributes to the growth of information about what does and does not succeed. As a corollary of choice, subsidized service provision by NPO's may segment society into many small groups, differentiated by religion or pedagogical ideology, rather than yielding the mixture found when most people use the government service. This is a "bad" to people who want integration, a "good" to those who prefer separation and pluralism.

4. *Regulation of subsidized nonprofits.*   In most cases when citizens support public subsidy of a service, they also have an interest in control to make sure they are getting what they paid for. Quantity, quality and the method of allocating the final product may all be important to voters, and the government is their agent (however imperfect) for carrying out their wishes. Accountability is facilitated if government produces the service, but this strategy can produce the inefficiencies just described. Alternatively, control can be exerted indirectly through regulations if production has been delegated to private organizations. Data from a variety of countries indicate that nonprofits do pay a price in terms of loss of autonomy as subsidies increase (James 1985, 1986b). By studying the nature of these regulations we can learn what can be monitored and what matters most to government and NPO's.

First of all, since inputs are readily observable while outputs (especially quality) are not, many regulations apply to inputs rather than outputs (James 1986b). For example, salaries, credentials and conditions of work are often set by the government and are similar to those of civil servants, once subsidies are instituted. This type of regulation is consistent with the hypothesis that government finance is a response to producer as well as consumer interests, so that many of the regulations are designed to protect the producers. It is paradoxical that NPO's may be subsidized because of an initial cost advantage but much of this cost advantage disappears after substantial subsidies are introduced.

Direct controls over certain output characteristics also exist, e.g. over curriculum and degree requirements in private schools. Controls extend, too, over the distribution of service, the criteria for selecting students, and the fees that can be charged in subsidized schools in many countries. Sometimes, private schools do not have the right to exclude students and must accept students assigned to them by the government. In the U.S., schools eligible for the implicit subsidy inherent in tax-exempt status may not follow segregationist admissions policies.

One of the most interesting regulations concerns the decision-making process in NPO's. Swedish NPO's are required to be "democratic" in order to qualify for subsidy; Dutch workers and consumers have a mandated role in the nonprofit decision-making structure. This is one way to maintain societal control yet permit decentralized production at the same time.

Thus, just as government faces a trade-off between efficiency and control, nonprofits face a trade-off between autonomy and more financial support. The equilibrium, in most cases, seems to involve a mixture of delegation and subsidy, with nonprofits retaining control over the service characteristics most important to them, such as ideological orientation. Some governments, however, choose complete control even if this means loss of efficiency and some nonprofits forego public funding in order to maintain their ideological purity.

B. Implicit tax subsidies

In the U.S. implicit tax subsidies play a very important role, much more so than in other parts of the world. Eligible NPO's are exempt from many taxes that ordinary businesses must pay, and contributions to them are tax-deductible. While the taxes themselves may be distortionary, eliminating them for one subset of organizations may be even more distortionary. Furthermore, the use of implicit rather than explicit subsidies decentralizes decision-making concerning which nonprofit activities will be supported and generally weakens the degree of central control. Thus, many of the above regulations that exist in other countries where direct grants prevail, are absent in the U.S.

1. *Tax deductible contributions.*   Under U.S. tax law individuals can deduct contributions to charitable organizations before calculating their level of taxable income. This system obviously lowers the effective price of charitable giving and provides relatively higher benefits to wealthy people in high marginal tax brackets. When marginal tax rates decline (as they have in recent years), the price of giving increases, therefore total donations may decline and the government pays (in terms of taxes foregone) a smaller share of the new total. Considerable empirical work has focused on the price elasticity of donations, which tells us whether individuals will then contribute more (inelastic) or less (elastic) of their own (after-tax) dollars. Most of these studies have found that the price elasticity of demand is greater then 1 in absolute value; i.e., if marginal tax rates decline, this causes over-all contributions to fall so much that NPO revenues fall by more than the government saves (Clotfelter and Salamon, 1982, Feldstein, 1975a, 1975b, Feldstein and Clotfelter, 1976, Feldstein and Taylor, 1976, Schiff, 1985, Clotfelter, 1985). Two studies, however, by Hood, Martin and Osberg (1977) and Reece and Zieschang (1985) have found price elasticities of less than one. Clotfelter and Steuerle (1981) and Auten and Rudney (1985) found low elasticities for some income groups using cross section data. Such elasticities imply that the drop in contributions when marginal tax rates fall is relatively modest, so that government saves more then NPO's lose in total philanthropic revenues. Reece and Zieschang argue that charitable giving tends to be a luxury that is more responsive to income than to price. For similarly conflicting analyses of estate taxation effects see Boskin (1976), who finds that charitable bequests are sensitive to tax rates, and Barthold and Plotnick (1984) who find that they are not.

More fundamental to our inquiry than estimates of price and income elasticity are attempts to justify the deduction and to assess the form that it takes. Since the deduction reduces the tax bills for those who donate to charity, we need to ask whether other taxes must increase as a consequence or whether the services provided through donations permit the government sector to be smaller than it otherwise would be. Even if the government budget is somewhat lower because of the existence of charitable substitutes, it is likely that the mix of services and their ideological composition is affected by the subsidy of donations. In particular, in the United States with its separation of church and state, donations to religious organizations are tax deductible. Without the deduction, religious organizations would be less well funded and some of the services they provide would be supplied by the state in an entirely secular manner.

In general, we would expect that gifts both raise the tax bills of non-givers and permit a lower public budget, but that even when substitution is important, the service mix will differ. Instead of reflecting majoritarian preferences, it will reflect the wishes of those who donate and of the nonprofit firms to which they contribute. Furthermore, given the present system of tax deductions, the pattern of service production is skewed toward the wishes of the relatively wealthy. Thus, under the current system, higher education and high culture are advantaged relative to religion because they are relatively attractive to high income donors. A shift to a tax credit (rather than tax deductibility), which many commentators favor as fairer because the marginal benefit of giving is independent of income class, would shift the balance toward the religious organizations favored by lower income people (Hochman and Rodgers, 1977). (Of course, any pattern of gifts can be counteracted by public budgetary policy and to some extent this does seem to happen. Government support is of greater relative importance for programs that aid the poor or that, like social security, cover a broad segment of the population than it is for private higher education or the arts).

The affirmative case for the subsidy of donations, then, sees them as a way to preserve and support ideological diversity and experimentation, especially in areas where government itself has no special claim to expertise (Simon, 1978). The government stimulus to gifts recognizes the public benefits that can be generated by private donations and provides an incentive to overcome free-rider problems. Critics of the deduction, in contrast, argue that government should only support activities on efficiency or majoritarian grounds, that it should not delegate the provision of social benefits to private organizations which may be inefficient, parochial, discriminatory, or elitist and that those unwilling to donate themselves should not have higher tax bills forced upon them because of a government policy of subsidizing gifts. Strnad (1986) counters by arguing that the deduction, whatever its effects, is the result of a political compromise that must have included a corresponding benefit for those harmed by the deduction.

2. *The corporate income tax exemption.* Similar claims and counterclaims can be made with respect to other forms of tax preferences, e.g. property tax exemptions and exemptions from the corporate income tax. But for these taxes another issue becomes important—the possibility of "unfair" competition between nonprofit and for-profit firms in the same industry.

Consider first the corporate income tax. In the U.S. nonprofits are exempt from this tax for all activities that are "related" to their basic functions. Thus the macaroni company once owned by New York University would not qualify but university cafeterias do. Is this efficient and is it fair? A tax levied as a percent of excess economic profits should have no behavioral implications in the short run for PMO's, since it does not affect the marginal conditions for profit maximization. However, as we saw in the section on profit constrained firms, it does affect behavior once arguments other than profits enter into the objective function via an income and substitution effect. It would affect nonprofit behavior even more.

Consider the choice between spending more on emoluments, staff, or high quality products on the one hand, versus maximizing net earnings on the other. The profit maximizing firm, by definition, would always choose the latter, regardless of the rate at which net earnings were taxed. The utility-maximizing firm, which cares about all these arguments, is initially spending more on emoluments, staff or quality than dictated by pure profit-maximization and the tax might exaggerate or diminish this tendency depending on whether the income or substitution effect predominates. The higher tax rate makes it cheaper to engage in "wasteful" spending, hence encourages it. On the other hand, the firm is anxious to maintain its after-tax earnings, either to pay dividends, to facilitate the raising of equity captial, or directly to finance future production. This mitigates the tendency of a profits tax to encourage wasteful spending, so the net impact is uncertain, probably small (and possibly even beneficial) in a utility-maximizing firm.

In a nonprofit, however, the first two mitigating factors (importance of dividends and equity capital) are irrelevant. Therefore, the nonprofit will almost certainly be induced to engage in more current "wasteful spending" if a profits tax is imposed, unless it has an urgent need to save for future activities. Thus, a tax on pure profits is not distortionary for a PMO, has little if any distortionary impact on a utility-maximizing firm, but is very likely to be distortionary for an NPO—an argument on intertemporal efficiency grounds for exempting nonprofits from such a tax.

Along similar lines, Hansmann (1981) shows that in a dynamic setting exemption from the corporate income tax can provide an important source of capital. He then justifies the NPO exemption as a way to compensate for their inability to raise equity capital. For him the exemption merely establishes NPO's on a more equal footing with PMO's.

Rose-Ackerman (1982b) concentrates on the tax on unrelated business profits. She argues that non-profits may, in fact, damage for-profit competitors if barriers to exit exist. However, these losses should only be of concern to policymakers if the PMO's would not have earned monopoly profits in the absence of NPO competition. She argues for the repeal of the unrelated business income tax on the ground that the tax concentrates NPO's profitmaking activities in a few "related" areas thus increasing the potential for harm to PMO's. Spread more broadly across the economy, these investments would be likely to have a minor impact.

3. *The property tax exemption.* Consider next the property tax. Since the property tax is a major source of income for local communities, the tax exemption is highly controversial in some areas that are heavily populated by nonprofits, e.g. Boston, New Haven and even New York. The Mayor of New York. at one point, proposed withdrawing this exemption on grounds that NPO's utilize local police and fire services but did not pay adequately for them; he was rebuffed on grounds that NPO's provided valuable cultural benefits and attracted many tax-paying people and businesses to the city. Of course, the same might be said of the for-profit Broadway theater, which is not tax exempt.

The tax exemption permits nonprofits to outbid comparable for-profits for valuable locations. If the firms are indeed in the same industry, producing the same product, then an entrepreneur might well choose the NPO form not for any public-spirited reason but simply in order to obtain a better location with lower taxes. If the industry is competitive so economic profits are zero, nonprofits drive for-profits out of business simply because of their tax advantage. If this scenario, in which organizational form depends purely on tax benefits, were empirically correct, there would be no principled justification for the benefits given to NPO's.

In practice, there are reasons to exempt at least some NPO's from this levy. Suppose that the nonprofit organization provides a community service but cannot capture all the benefits of its location through entry fees or charges; like a church or library, it may not have any admission charge at all. However, the level of public benefits is positively related to the centrality of its location and well-located property is expensive. Thus the government, to the extent that it supports the objectives of the organization, may wish to subsidize its location costs.

This, however, is an argument for subsidizing land rent or for using zoning ordinances to set aside some land for publicly desirable purposes. It is not an argument for a general tax exemption that includes real property. Unless nonprofit capital is especially likely to create positive externalities, e.g. a beautiful church or museum building, there does not seem to be any particular reason to choose property tax exemption as the form of aid as opposed to direct subsidy. From a positive point of view, a property tax subsidy may be used because it is less visible and more automatic than a direct grant and thus seems to involve the public sector less. From a normative point of view, the case for choosing this subsidy mechanism is weak.

C. Cross-subsidization

One of the more controversial aspects of NPO funding concerns the practice of cross-subsidization. Is this a desirable practice? Should it be permitted, encouraged, or prohibited by public policy? Since nonprofits are given a variety of tax privileges, as well as legal monopolies and rights to exclude competitors, (e.g. self-regulatory accrediting boards in higher education and legalized bingo for church groups), all of which facilitate profits and cross-subsidization, it is reasonable to ask about the efficiency and equity of the outcome.

We have seen that cross-subsidization creates a divergence between NPO and PMO behavior whenever there are potential profits, i.e. except in long run competitive equilibrium with zero donations or entry barriers. It follows that, in situations where PMO production is optimal, NPO production will generally be nonoptimal, because of cross-subsidization. Specifically, if $(P_i + D_i)$, price plus donations per unit of good i, represents society's marginal valuation of good i, organizational consumption (utility-yielding) activities will be underproduced and production-negative consumption (disutility-yielding) activities will be underproduced by NPO's. For example, if undergraduates at nonprofit universities are profitable and graduate students are subsidized, enrollment decisions of students do not automatically take real costs into account. Too few undergraduates and too many graduate students may choose to enroll at universities, particularly if demand is elastic. Similarly, the supply of potential faculty members is more abundant than it would be if graduate students paid for their full education, the faculty wage therefore understates its real (training) cost, and the use of physical capacity by colleges and universities is discouraged in favor of (seemingly) cheap human capital, by these false price signals.

As discussed earlier, however, nonprofits may operate precisely in those fields where positive externalities or monitoring problems exist, so that $(P_i + D_i)$ understates the true social marginal benefit; at least, that is the presumption behind the "public goods" and "contract failure" theories of nonprofit formation. In that case, the profit-maximizing output (or quality) would be too low, and a nonprofit manager with a preference for such a good would move us closer toward efficiency. For example, if the benefits of research are substantial, and neither individuals nor state legislators will voluntarily finance an optimal amount, because of nonexcludability problems, society at large gains when universities divert resources to research activities (and to graduate programs which train students to do research). Cross-subsidization is than seen as a "second best" solution, an alternative funding mechanism to the national government budget, avoiding many of the disincentive and informational problems inherent in taxes and central planning.

Welfare may then be improved by turning decision-making about resource allocation over to NPO managers with the "right" objective functions who, by their choice of product mix and technology, are simply "protecting the public interest." (Of course, there is no guarantee that their objective functions are, in fact, "right.")

Besides these efficiency considerations, cross-subsidization has been questioned on equity or procedural grounds. The current procedure implicitly increases the real income of NPO managers who have been assigned discretionary "property rights" over the input and output mix of their organization, without the discipline and limits imposed by either competitive or regulated markets. It also redistributes income from one set of customers to another, i.e. from consumers of profitable activities to consumers of loss-making activities, by making the latter goods available below cost. This maximizes the manager's objective function but may not be consistent with society's concept of distributional equity. Indeed, nonprofit hospital managers have been attacked, on precisely these grounds, as constituting "an undemocratic ruling class [employing] an unjust method of taxation . . ." (Clark 1980, pp. 1439, 1465).

In addition, donors may be misled about the marginal impact of their gifts on the organization's behavior if they do not know about the pattern of cross-subsidization. If indeed misinformation is the problem, one possible remedy is full disclosure—of costs and revenues, profitable and loss-making goods. However, the difficulties in prohibiting cross-subsidization or in requiring full disclosure should not be minimized. Many products of NPO's are jointly produced, so calculation of their separate costs would be difficult and, ultimately, arbitrary. NPO industries typically contain many small units, each of which would have to go through an elaborate cost analysis, in contrast to regulated public utilities, which are much more highly concentrated and can therefore analyze their costs with less duplication.

Finally, we must acknowledge that the concept of "equity" is highly subjective. All people would not agree on whether the income distribution is made better or worse after cross-subsidization by NPO's. The delegation of some discretion about real income to NPO's and other organizations which are partially immune to both market and political forces may reflect the inability of a heterogeneous society to agree on what equity is and our unwillingness to choose a single mechanism for making decisions about income distribution.

D. Conclusion

Private nonprofit firms stand between government agencies and profit-maximizing firms. Like the PMO, the NPO relies to a large extent on voluntary payments and hence must provide services that appeal to potential clients (donors and customers). Like the government, it does not distribute a monetary residual and hence lacks strong incentives for efficiency. Furthermore, the existence of revenues that are not contingent upon product sales (donations, subsidies) enable it to pursue some of the objectives usually associated with the public sector (such as provision of quasi-public goods and income redistribution). Unlike either government bureaus or PMO's, the NPO's pursue a wide range of ideological (religious) goals, and their fundraising and product variety consequently have an ideological dimension.

We have tried in this review essay to take a realistic view of the strengths and weaknesses of nonprofit organizations relative to both for-profit firms and public agencies, based on theoretical models and on empirical tests. The result is, we hope, a balanced assessment that affirms the continuing importance of NPO's in many sectors of the economy while avoiding exaggerated claims for their overriding value. The NPO name itself simply announces a constraint—the firm has no owners able to appropriate any surplus generated by the firm. This is an important constraint but it can be vitiated by a strong competitive environment, by managers who either engage in outright fraud and shirking or simply have strong beliefs that run counter to the wishes of donors and paying customers. As in the analysis of bureaucracies and for-profit firms, agency-principal problems are at the heart of the analysis of NPO behavior and one's evaluation of the performance of the sector frequently depends on whose point of view one takes. What one person views as inefficient, self-indulgent or diverse behavior by NPO managers, another views as socially beneficial, admirably generous or a reflection of the ideological diversity of the population.

Bibliography

Abrams, Burton A. and Mark D. Schmitz. "The Crowding-out Effect of Transfers on Private Charitable Contributions," *Public Choice* (1978) **33**, 29–40. Reprinted in Rose-Ackerman, ed. *The Economics of Nonprofit Institutions: Studies in Structure and Policy*, N.Y.: Oxford University Press, 1986.

Akerlof, George. "The Market for Lemons," *Quarterly J. of Economics* (August 1970) **17**, 488–500.

Alchian, Armen A. and Harold Demsetz. "Production, Information Costs, and Economic Organization," *American Economic Review* (Dec. 1972) **62**, 777–795.

Alchian, Armen and Reuben Kessel. "Competition, Monopoly, and the Pursuit of Pecuniary 'Gains'" *Aspects of Labor Economics* (1962) Princeton: NBER.

American Association of Fundraising Council. *Giving USA,* New York 1981.

Arnold, R. Douglas. *Congress and the Bureaucracy,* New Haven: Yale University Press, 1979.

Arrow, Kenneth. "Gifts and Exchanges," *Philosophy and Public Affairs* (Summer 1974) **3**, 343–362.

Auten, Gerald E. and Gabriel Rudney. "Tax Policy and Its Impact on the High Income Giver," Independent Sector Research Forum, (1985) 525–545.

Balderston, F. *Managing Today's University* San Francisco: Jossey-Bass, 1974.

Barthold, Thomas and Robert Plotnick. "Estate Taxtion and Other Determinants of Charitable Bequests," *National Tax J.* (June 1984) **37**, 225–237.

Baumol, William J. *Business Behavior Value and Growth* revised edition, New York: Harcourt, Brace, 1967.

Baumol, William J. "Toward a Theory of Public Enterprise," C. V. Starr Center for Applied Economics, New York University, (August 1983) 26.

Bays, Carson W. "Cost Comparisons of Forprofit and Nonprofit Hospitals," *Social Science and Medicine* (1979) 13.

Bays, Carson W. "Why Most Private Hospitals Are Nonprofit." *J. of Policy Analysis and Management* (Spring 1983) **2**, 266–285.

Becker, Gary. "Altruism, Egoism and Genetic Fitness: Economics and Sociobiology," *J. of Econ. Lit.* (Sept. 1976) **14**, 817–826.

Ben-Ner, Avner. "Nonprofit Collectivist Organizations," in W. Powell, ed. *Between the Public and the Private: The Nonprofit Sector.* New Haven: Yale University Press, 1986.

Ben-Ner, Avner. "Nonprofit Organizations: Why do they Exist in Market Economies?," in Rose-Ackerman, ed. *The Economics of Nonprofit Institutions: Studies in Structure and Policy*, N.Y.: Oxford University Press, 1986.

Blair, Roger, Paul Ginsburg and Ronald Vogel. "Blue Cross-Blue Shield Administration Costs: A Study of Nonprofit Health Insurers." *Economic Inquiry* (June 1975) **13**, 237–251.

Boskin, Michael. "Estate Taxation and Charitable Bequests," *J. of Public Economics* (1976) **5**, 27–56.

Breton, A. and R. Wintrobe. "The Equilibrium Size of a Budget Maximizing Bureau," *Journal of Political Economy* (February 1975) **83**, 185–207.

Breton, A. and R. Wintrobe. *The Logic of Bureaucratic Conduct,* Cambridge: Cambridge University Press, 1982.

Clark, Robert. "Does the Nonprofit Form Fit the Hospital Industry?" *Harvard Law Review* (May 1980) **93**, 1416–1489.

Clarkson, Kenneth. "Some Implications of Property Rights in Hospital Management," *Journal of Law and Economics,* (1972), **15**, 363–384.

Clarkson, Kenneth and Donald Martin, eds. *The Economics of Nonproprietary Organizations,* Greenwich, Conn.: JAI Press, 1980.

Clotfelter, Charles. *Federal Tax Policy and Charitable Giving,* Chicago: University of Chicago Press, 1985.

Clotfelter, Charles and Lester Salamon. "The Impact of the 1981 Tax Act on Individual Charitable Giving." *National Tax Journal* (June 1982) **35,** 171–1787. Reprinted in Rose-Ackerman, ed. *The Economics of Nonprofit Institutions: Studies in Structure and Policy,* N.Y.: Oxford University Press, 1986.

Clotfelter, Charles and C. Eugene Steuerle. "Charitable Contributions" in Aaron and Pechman, eds., *How Taxes Affect Economic Behavior,* Washington, D.C.: Brookings Inst., 1981, pp. 403–446.

Cohn, Elchanan. *The Economics of Education,* Cambridge, Mass.: Ballinger, 1975, pp. 240–269.

Collard, David. *Altruism and Economy: A Study in Non-Selfish Economics,* N.Y.: Oxford University Press, 1978.

Daly, George and J. Fred Giertz. "Benevolence, Malevolence and Economic Theory," *Public Choice* (Fall 1972) **13,** 1–19.

Danielsen, Albert L. "A Theory of Exchange, Philanthropy and Appropriation," *Public Choice* (1975) **24,** 13–26.

Easley, David and Maureen O'Hara. "Optimal Nonprofit Firms," in Rose-Ackerman, ed. *The Economics of Nonprofit Institutions: Studies in Structure and Policy,* N.Y.: Oxford University Press, 1986.

Easley, David and Maureen O'Hara. "The Economic Role of Nonprofit Firms," *Bell J. of Econ.* (Autumn 1983) **14,** 531–538.

Fama, Eugene and Michael Jensen. "Agency Problems and Residual Claims," *J. of Law and Economics* (June 1983a) **26,** 327–250.

Fama, Eugene and Michael Jensen. "Separation of Ownership and Control," *J. of Law and Economics* (June 1983b) **26,** 301–326.

Feigenbaum, Susan. "The Case of Income Redistribution: A Theory of Government and Private Provision of Collective Goods," *Public Finance Quarterly* (1980) **8,** 3–22.

Feigenbaum, Susan. "Competition and Performance in the Nonprofit Sector: The Case of Medical Research Charities," mimeo, (1983).

Feldstein, Martin. "The Income Tax and Charitable Contributions: Part I—Aggregate and Distributional Effects," *National Tax Journal,* (1975a), **28,** 81–100.

Feldstein, Martin. "The Income Tax and Charitable Contributions: Part II—The Impact on Religious, Educational, and Other Organizations," *National Tax Journal,* (1975b) **28**.

Feldstein, Martin and Charles Clotfelter. "Tax Incentives and Charitable Contributions in the United States," *Journal of Public Economics,* (1976) **5,** 1–26.

Feldstein, Martin and Amy Taylor. "The Income Tax and Charitable Contributions," *Econometrica* (Nov. 1976) **44,** 1201–1222.

Fiorina, Morris and Roger Noll. "Voters, Legislators and Bureaucracy: Institutional Design in the Public Sector," *American Economic Review—Papers and Proceedings* (May 1978) **68,** 256–260.

Fisher, Franklin. "On Donor Sovereignty and United Charities," *Am. Econ. Review* (September 1977) **67,** 632–638.

Frech, H. E. III. "Health Insurance: Private, Mutual, or Government." In Clarkson and Martin, eds. *The Economics of Nonproprietary Organizations,* Greenwich, CT: JAI Press. 1980.

Frech, H. E. III. "The Property Rights Theory of the Firm: Empirical Results from a Natural Experiment," *Journal of Political Economy*, (1976) **84**, 143–152.
Frech, H. E. III and P. Ginsburg. "Competition Among Insurers" in W. Greenberg, ed. *Competition in the Health Care Sector: Past, Present and Future*, 1978.
Geiger, Roger. *Private Sectors in High Education: Structure, Function and Change in Eight Countries*, mimeo, 1984.
Geiger, Roger and P. Ginsburg. "Property Rights and Competition in Health Insurance: Multiple Objectives for Nonprofit Firms," *Research in Law and Economics* (1981) **3**, 155–172.
Gertler, Paul. "Structural and Behavioral Differences in the Performance of Proprietary and 'Not for Profit' Organizations," mimeo, (1984).
Hansmann, Henry. "Economic Theories of Nonprofit Organizations," in W. Powell, ed. *Between the Public and the Private: The Nonprofit Sector*, New Haven: Yale University Press, 1986.
Hansmann, Henry. "The Effect of Tax Exemption and Other Factors on Competitive Organizations," Yale University, PONPO Workshop paper No. 65, 1982.
Hansmann, Henry. "Nonprofit Enterprise in the Performing Arts," *Bell J. of Economics* (Autumn 1981) **12**, 341–361.
Hansmann, Henry. "The Rationale for Exempting Nonprofit Organizations from the Corporate Income Tax," *Yale L. J.* (November 1981) **91**, 54–100. Reprinted in Rose-Ackerman, ed. *The Economics of Nonprofit Institutions: Studies in Structure and Policy*, N.Y.: Oxford University Press, 1986.
Hansmann, Henry. "The Role of Non-Profit Enterprise," *Yale L. J.* (April 1980) **89**, 835–898. Reprinted in Rose-Ackerman, ed. *The Economics of Nonprofit Institutions: Studies in Structure and Policy*, N.Y.: Oxford University Press, 1986.
Hirshleifer, Jack. "Competition, Cooperation and Conflict in Economics and Biology," *Amer. Econ. Review* (May 1978) **68**, 238–243.
Hochman, Harold, and James Rodgers. "The Optimal Tax Treatment of Charitable Contributions." *National Tax J.* (March 1977) **30**, 1–19. Reprinted in Rose-Ackerman, ed. *The Economics of Nonprofit Institutions: Studies in Structure and Policy*, N.Y.: Oxford University Press, 1986.
Hochman, Harold and James Rodgers. "Pareto Optimal Redistribution." *American Economic Review* (September 1969) **59**, 542–557.
Hochman, Harold, and James Rodgers. "Utility Interdependence and Income Transfers Through Charity," in K. Boulding and M. Pfaff, eds., *Transfers in an Urbanized Economy: Theories and Effects of the Grants Economy*, Belmont, California: Wadsworth, 1973.
Hodgkinson, Virginia and M. Weitzman. *The Dimensions of the Nonprofit Sector*, Independent Sector, Washington, D.C. 1984.
Holtmann, A. G. "A Theory of Non-Profit Firms," *Economica* (1983) **50**, 439–449.
Hood, R. D., S. A. Martin and L. S. Osberg. "Economic Determinants of Individual Charitable Donations in Canada," *Canadian J. of Economics* (Nov. 1977) **10**, 653–669.
Ireland, Thomas R., and David B. Johnson. *The Economics of Charity*. Center for the Study of Public Choice, Blacksburg, Virginia, 1970.
James, Estelle. "Benefits and Costs of Privatized Public Services: Lessons from the Dutch Educational System," *Comparative Education Review*, (1984a) **28**, 605–625. Reprinted in Levy, ed. *Private Education: Studies in Choice and Public Policy*, NY: Oxford University Press, 1986.
James, Estelle. "Cross Subsidization in Higher Education: Does it Pervert Private

96   E. JAMES AND S. ROSE-ACKERMAN

Choice and Public Policy?" in Levy, ed., *Private Education: Studies in Choice and Public Policy,* NY: Oxford University Press, 1986a.

James, Estelle. "How Nonprofits Grow: A Model," *J. of Policy Analysis and Management* (Spring 1983) **2,** 350–365. Reprinted in Rose-Ackerman, ed. *The Economics of Nonprofit Institutions: Studies in Structure and Policy,* N.Y.: Oxford University Press, 1986.

James, Estelle. "The Nonprofit Sector in Comparative Perspective," in Walter Powell, ed. *Between the Public and the Private: The Not-for-Profit Sector,* New Haven: Yale University Press, 1986b.

James, Estelle. "The Nonprofit Sector in International Perspective: The Case of Sri Lanka," *J. of Comparative Economics* (June 1982a) **6,** 99–129.

James, Estelle. "The Private Nonprofit Provision of Education: A Theoretical Model and Application to Japan," *J. of Comparative Economics* (1986c) 10.

James, Estelle. "The Private Provision of Public Services: A Comparison of Sweden and Holland," Yale University, PONPO Working Paper # 60 (1982b).

James, Estelle. "Product Mix and Cost Disaggregation: A Reinterpretation of the Economics of Higher Education," *Journal of Human Resources* (1978) **13,** 157–86.

James, Estelle. "The Public/Private Division of Responsibility for Education: An International Comparison," paper presented at the IFG Conference on Public and Private Education, Stanford University, (October 1984b).

James, Estelle. "Public Subsidies in the Private Nonprofit Sector," Independent Sector Research Forum, 1985.

James, Estelle and Gail Benjamin. "Public versus Private education: The Japanese Experiment," Yale University, PONPO Working Paper # 81 (1984).

James, Estelle and Egon Neuberger. "The University Department as a Nonprofit Labor Cooperative," *Public Choice* (1981) **36,** 585–612.

Jensen, Michael and William Meckling. "Theory of the Firm: Managerial Behavior, Agency Costs and Ownership Structure," *J. Financial Economics* (1976) **3,** 305–360.

Jones, P. R. "Aid to Charities," *International J. of Social Economics* (1983, No. 2) **10,** 3–12.

Katzmann, Robert. *Regulatory Bureaucracies,* Cambridge, Mass: MIT Press, 1980.

Kaufman, Herbert. *The Administrative Behavior of Federal Bureau Chiefs,* Washington, D.C.: Brookings Institution, 1981.

Kramer, Ralph. *Voluntary Agencies in the Welfare State* Berkeley: University of California Press, 1981.

Krashinsky, Michael. "Transactions Cost and a Look at the Nonprofit Organization," in Rose-Ackerman, ed. *The Economics of Nonprofit Institutions: Studies in Structure and Policy,* N.Y.: Oxford University Press, 1986.

Lee, A. James and Burton Weisbrod. "Collective Goods and the Voluntary Sector: The Case of the Hospital Industry," in Burton Weisbrod, *The Voluntary Nonprofit Sector,* Lexington, MA: D.C. Heath & Co. 1977.

Lee, M. L. "A Conspicuous Production Theory of Hospital Behavior." *Southern Economic Journal* (July 1971) **38,** 48–59.

Legoretta, Judith M. and Dennis Young. "Why Organizations Turn Nonprofit: Lessons from Case Studies," in S. Rose-Ackerman, ed. *The Economics of Nonprofit Institutions: Studies in Structure and Policy,* N.Y.: Oxford University Press, 1986.

Leibenstein, Harvey. "Allocative Efficiency vs. 'X-Efficiency.'" *American Economic Review* (June 1966) **56,** 392–415.

Levy, Daniel, ed. *Private Education: Studies in Choice and Public Policy*, NY: Oxford University Press, 1986.

Levy, Daniel, *The State and Higher Education in Latin America*, Chicago: University of Chicago Press, 1986.

Levy, F. K. "Economic Analysis of the Nonprofit Institution—The Case of the Private University." *Public Choice* (Spring 1968) **4**, 3–17.

Lindsay, Cotton. "A Theory of Government Enterprise." *Journal of Political Economy* (October, 1976) **84**, 1061–77.

Long, Stephen H. "Social Pressure and Contributions to Health Charities," *Public Choice* (Winter, 1976) **28**, 55–66.

Margolis, Howard, *Selfishness, Altruism and Rationality*, New York: Cambridge University Press, 1982.

Mashaw, Jerry L. *Bureaucratic Justice: Managing Social Security Disability Claims*, New Haven: Yale University Press, 1983.

McGuire, Martin. "Private Good Clubs and Public Good Clubs: Economic Models of Group Formation." *Swedish Journal of Economics* (1972) **74**, 84–99.

Melnick, R. S. *Regulation and the Courts: The Case of the Clean Air Act*, Washington, D.C.: Brookings Inst., 1983.

Migue, J. L. and G. Belanger. "Toward a General Theory of Managerial Discretion," *Public Choice* (Spring, 1974) **17**, 27–47.

Montias, J. M. "Public Support for the Performing Arts in Western Europe and the U.S.: History and Analysis," in M. Leiserson, C. Taft Morris and G. Ranis, eds. *Comparative Development Perspective*, Boulder, Col.: Westview, 1984.

Moran, Mark and Barry Weingast. "Bureaucratic Discretion or Congressional Control," *J. Pol. Econ.* **91**, 765–800 (1983).

Nelson, Richard and Michael Krashinsky. "Two Major Issues of Policy: Public Subsidy and Organization of Supply," in D. Young and R. Nelson, eds., *Public Policy for Day Care of Young Children*, Lexington, Mass: D.C. Heath, 1973.

Neuberger, Egon and Estelle James. "The Yugoslav Self-Managed Enterprise—A Systemic Approach," in M. Bornstein, ed. *Plan and Market*, New Haven: Yale University Press, 1973, pp. 245–284.

Newhouse, Joseph. "Toward a Theory of Nonprofit Institutions: An Economic Model of a Hospital." *American Economic Review* (March 1970) **60**, 64–73.

Niskanen, William. *Bureaucracy and Representative Government*, Chicago: Aldine-Atherton, 1971.

Niskanen, William. "Bureaucrats and Politicians," *Journal of Law and Economics* (December 1975) **18**, 617–644.

O'Donoghue, M. *Economic Dimensions in Education*, Chicago: Aldine 1971.

Pauly, Mark and Michael Redisch. "The Not-for-Profit Hospital as a Physicians' Cooperative," *American Economic Review*, (1973) **63**, 87–99.

Permut, Steven. "Consumer Perception of Nonprofit Enterprise: A Comment on Hansmann," *Yale L.J.* (June 1981) **91**, 1623–32.

Phelps, Edmund S., ed. *Altruism, Morality and Economic Theory*, New York: Russell Sage Foundation, 1975.

Pigou, A. C. *The Economics of Welfare*, Fourth Edition, London: Macmillan, 1948.

Posner, Richard. "Theories of Economic Regulation," *Bell J. of Economics.* (1974) **5**, 335–358.

Powell, Walter W., ed. *Between the Public and the Private: The Nonprofit Sector*, New Haven: Yale University Press, 1986.

Preston, Ann. "The Nonprofit Firm: A Potential Solution to Inherent Market

Failure," Wellesley College Department of Economics, Working Paper No. 77, 1984a.

Preston, Ann. "The Nonprofit Worker in a For-profit World," Wellesley College, Manuscript, 1984b.

Preston, Ann. "Women in the White Collar Nonprofit Sector: The Best Option or the Only Option," Wellesley College, Manuscript, 1985.

Reece, William and Kimberly Zieschang. "Consistent Estimation of the Impact of Tax Deductibility on the Level of Charitable Contributions," *Econometrica* (March 1985) **53**, 271–293.

Roberts, Russell D. "A Positive Model of Private Charity and Public Transfers," *J. of Political Economy* (February 1984) **92**, 136–148.

Rose-Ackerman, Susan. "Charitable Giving and 'Excessive' Fundraising," *Quarterly Journal of Economics* (May 1982a) **97**, 195–212. Reprinted in Rose-Ackerman, ed. *The Economics of Nonprofit Institutions: Studies in Structure and Policy*, N.Y.: Oxford University Press, 1986.

Rose-Ackerman, Susan. *Corruption: A Study in Political Economy*, New York: Academic Press, 1978.

Rose-Ackerman, Susan. "Do Government Grants to Charity Reduce Private Donations?" *Nonprofit Firms in a Three Sector Economy* (M. White, ed.), 95–114, 1981 Reprinted in Rose-Ackerman, ed. *The Economics of Nonprofit Institutions: Studies in Structure and Policy*, N.Y.: Oxford University Press, 1986.

Rose-Ackerman, Susan, ed. *The Economics of Nonprofit Institutions: Studies in Structure and Policy*, N.Y.: Oxford University Press, 1986.

Rose-Ackerman, Susan, "Reforming Public Bureaucracy through Economic Incentives?," *U. of Law, Economics and Organization* (Spring 1986) **2**, 131–161.

Rose-Ackerman, Susan. "Social Services and the Market," *Columbia Law Review* (October 1983b) **83**, 1405–1438.

Rose-Ackerman, Susan. "Tiebout Models and the Competitive Ideal: An Essay on the Political Economy of Local Government," in John Quigley, ed. *Perspectives on Local Public Finance and Public Policy*, Volume 1., Greenwich, CT: JAI Press Inc., 1983c, pp. 23–46.

Rose-Ackerman, Susan. "Unfair Competition and Corporate Income Taxation," *Standord L. Review* (May 1982b) **34**, 1017–1039. Reprinted in Rose-Ackerman, ed. *The Economics of Nonprofit Institutions: Studies in Structure and Policy*, N.Y.: Oxford University Press, 1986.

Rose-Ackerman, Susan. "Unintended Consequences: Regulating the Quality of Subsidized Day Care," *J. of Policy Analysis and Management* (Fall 1983a) **3**, 14–30.

Rose-Ackerman, Susan. "United Charities: An Economic Analysis," *Public Policy* (Summer 1980) **28**, 323–350.

Salamon, Lester. "Nonprofit Organizations: The Lost Opportunity," in J. Palmer and I. Sawhill, eds. *The Reagan Record*, Cambridge, Mass.: Ballinger, 1984, 261–286.

Salamon, Lester and Alan Abramson. *The Federal Budget and the Nonprofit Sector*, Washington D.C.: Urban Institute, 1982.

Schiff, Jerald. "Does Government Spending Crowd Out Charitable Contributions?," Tulane University, New Orleans, manuscript November 1984.

Schiff, Jerald. "Tax Reform and Charitable Giving: What Do We Really Know," Tulane University, March 1985.

Schlesinger, Mark. "Economic Models of Nonprofit Organizations: A Reappraisal of the Property Rights Approach," presented at the A.E.A. Meetings, 1985.

Schlesinger, Mark and Robert Dorwart. "Ownership and Mental-Health Services: A

Reappraisal of the Shift toward Privately Owned Facilities," *New England J. of Medicine* (October 11, 1984) **311,** 959–965.

Seaman, Bruce A. "Local Subsidization of Culture: A Public Choice Model Based on Household Utility Maximization," *J. of Behavioral Economics* (Summer 1979) **8,** 93–131.

Simon, John. "Charity and Dynasty Under the Federal Tax System." *The Probate Lawer* vol. 5 (Summer 1978). Reprinted in Rose-Ackerman, ed. *The Economics of Nonprofit Institutions: Studies in Structure and Policy,* N.Y.: Oxford University Press, 1986.

Skloot, Edward. "Enterprise and Commerce in Nonprofit Organizations," in Walter Powell, ed. *Between the Public and the Private: The Nonprofit Sector,* New Haven: Yale University Press, 1986.

Smith, Bruce and Nelson Rosenbaum. "The Fiscal Capacity of the Voluntary Sector," paper prepared for the Brookings Institution National Issues Seminar on "The Response of the Private Sector to Government Retrenchment," Washington, D.C. December 9, 1981.

Smith, Sharon P. *Equal Pay in the Public Sector: Fact or Fantasy* Princeton, N.J.: Industrial Relations Section, Princeton University, 1977.

Spence, Michael. "Product Selection, Fixed Costs and Monopolistic Competition," *Review of Economic Studies* **43,** 217–235 (1976).

Steinberg, Richard. "Nonprofit Organizations and the Market," in Walter Powell, ed. *Between the Public and the Private: The Nonprofit Sector,* New Haven: Yale University Press, 1986a.

Steinberg, Richard. "Should Donors Care About Fundraising?," in Rose-Ackerman, ed. *The Economics of Nonprofit Institutions: Studies in Structure and Policy,* N.Y.: Oxford University Press, 1986b.

Steinwald, Bruce and Duncan Neuhauser. "The Role of the Proprietary Hospital," *Law and Contemporary Problems* (Autumn 1970) **35,** 817–838.

Strnad II, James F. "The Charitable Contribution Deduction: A Political Economic Analysis," in Rose-Ackerman, ed. *The Economics of Nonprofit Institutions: Studies in Structure and Policy,* N.Y.: Oxford University Press, 1986.

Sugden, Robert. "Reciprocity: The Supply of Public Goods Through Voluntary Contributions," *Economic Journal* (Dec. 1984) **94,** 772–787.

Tanaka, Minoru and Takako Ameniya. *Philanthropy in Japan '83: Private Nonprofit Activities in Japan,* Tokyo: Japan Assoc. of Charitable Organizations, 1983.

Thompson, Earl A. "Charity and Nonprofit Organizations," in Clarkson and Martin, ed. *The Economics of Nonproprietary Organizations* Greenwich: JAI Press, 1980, 125–138.

Titmus, Richard. *The Gift Relationship,* N.Y.: Pantheon, 1971.

Tullock, Gordon. "The Charity of the Uncharitable." *Western Economic Journal,* (December 1971) **4,** 379–392.

Tullock, Gordon. "Information Without Profit," in G. Tullock, ed. *Papers on Non-Market Decision Making,* Thomas Jefferson Center for Political Economy, Univ. of Virginia, 1966, pp. 141–159.

Viscusi, Kip W. "Presidential Oversight: Controlling the Regulators," *J. of Policy Analysis and Management* (Winter 1983) **2,** 157–173.

Vogel, Ronald, "The Effects of Taxation on the Differential Efficiency of Nonprofit Health Insurance." *Economic Inquiry* (October 1977) **15,** 605–609.

Weisbrod, Burton. "Nonprofit and Proprietary Sector Behavior: Wage Differentials Among Lawyers," *Journal of Labor Economics* **4,** 246–263 (1983).

Weisbrod, Burton. *The Not-for-Profit Sector in a Mixed Economy,* Manuscript, Twentieth Century Fund, N.Y., 1985.

Weisbrod, Burton. "Private Goods, Collective Goods: The Role of the Nonprofit Sector," in Clarkson and Martin, eds. *The Economics of Nonproprietary Organizations* Greenwich: JAI Press, 1980, 139–169.

Weisbrod, Burton. "Toward a Theory of the Voluntary Nonprofit Sector in a Three-Sector Economy," in Burton Weisbrod, ed., *The Voluntary Nonprofit Sector*, Lexington, Mass.: D. C. Heath, 1977 51–76. Reprinted in Rose-Ackerman, ed. *The Economics of Nonprofit Institutions: Studies in Structure and Policy*, N.Y.: Oxford University Press, 1986.

Weisbrod, Burton with Joel Handler and Neil Komesar. *Public Interest Law* Berkeley: University of California Press, 1978.

Weisbrod, Burton and Mark Schlesinger. "Ownership Form and Behavior in Regulated Markets with Asymmetric Information," in Rose-Ackerman, ed. *The Economics of Nonprofit Institutions: Studies in Structure and Policy*, N.Y.: Oxford University Press, 1986.

Weisbrod, Burton and Nestor Dominguez, "Demand for Collective Goods in Private Nonprofit Markets: Can Fundraising Expenditures Help Overcome Free Rider Behavior?" *Journal of Public Economics* (1986).

Weiss, Jeffrey. "Donations: Can They Reduce a Donor's Welfare?," in Rose-Ackerman, ed. *The Economics of Nonprofit Institutions: Studies in Structure and Policy*, N.Y.: Oxford University Press, 1986.

White, Michelle, ed. *Nonprofit Firms in a Three Sector Economy*, COUPE paper on Public Economic No. 6, Washington, D.C.: Urban Institute, 1981.

Williamson, Oliver. *The Economics of Discretionary Behavior: Managerial Objectives in a Theory of the Firm*, Englewood Cliffs: Prentice-Hall, 1964.

Williamson, Oliver. *Markets and Hierarchies*, New York: Free Press, 1975.

Wintrobe, Ronald. "It Pays to Do Good, but Not to Do More Good than it Pays," *J. of Econ. Behavior and Organization* (1981) **2**, 201–213.

Wintrobe, Ronald. "Taxing Altruism," *Econ. Inquiry* (April 1983) **21**, 255–270.

Young, Dennis. *Casebook of Management for Nonprofit Organizations: Entrepreneurship and Organizational Change in the Human Services*, N.Y.: Haworth Press, 1985.

Young Dennis. "Entrepreneurship and the Behavior of Nonprofit Organizations: Elements of a Theory," in M. White, 1981. Reprinted in Rose-Ackerman, ed. *The Economics of Nonprofit Institutions: Studies in Structure and Policy*, N.Y.: Oxford University Press, 1986.

Young, Dennis. *If Not for Profit, for What?*, Lexington, Mass.: D. C. Heath, 1983.

INDEX